Pea MATHEMATICS

Level 2b

Stage 5

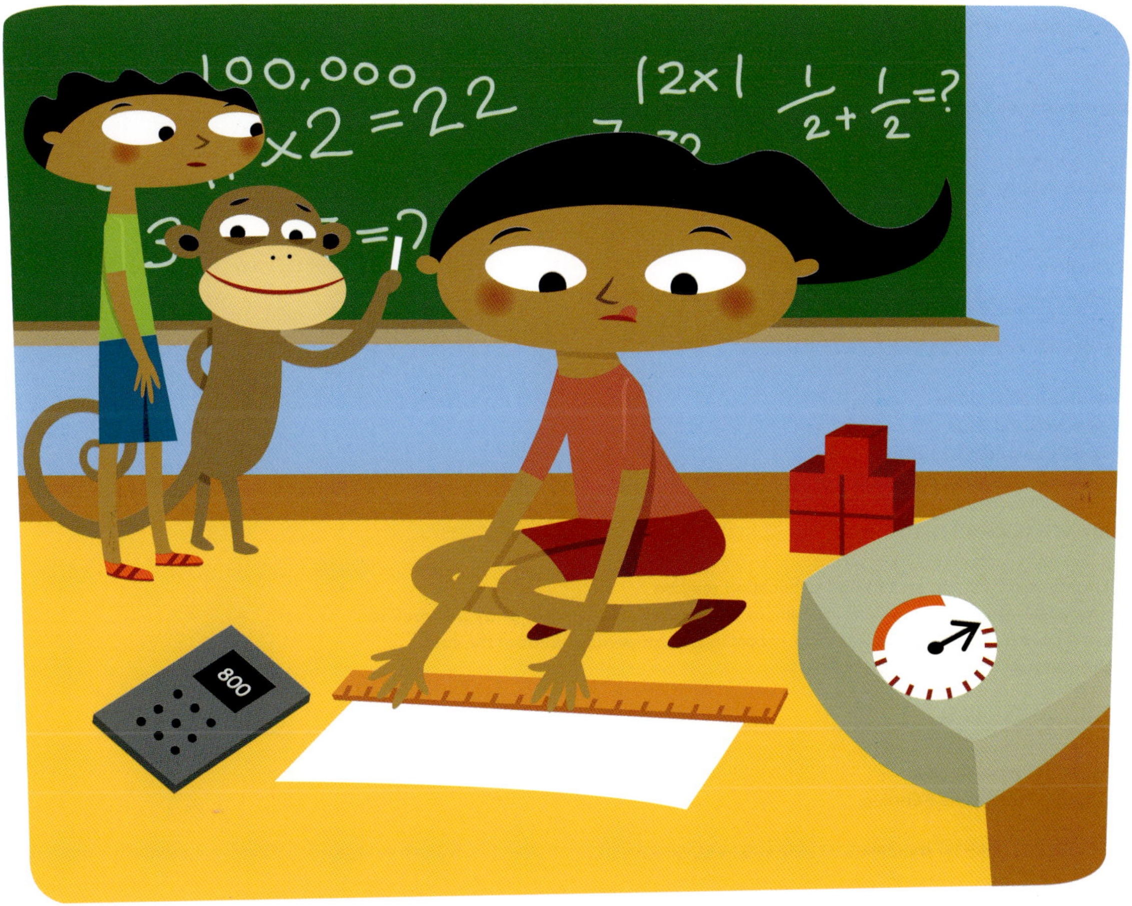

Charlotte Wilkinson

PEARSON

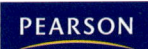

Acknowledgements:
The publisher would like to thank
Charles McKenzie, Charlotte Wilkinson,
Mark Glover and Donna Mataira for supplying
many of the photographs in this book.

Other photographs: PhotoDisc, iStockphoto and Dreamstime

www.pearsoned.co.nz

Your comments on this book are welcome at
feedback@pearsoned.co.nz

Pearson
a division of Pearson New Zealand Ltd
67 Apollo Drive, Rosedale, Auckland 0632, New Zealand

Associated companies throughout the world

© Pearson 2000, 2009
First published 2000
This edition published 2009
Reprinted 2010 (x2), 2011, 2012

ISBN: 978-1-44250-592-6

Produced by Pearson

Illustrator: Karen Oppatt
Designer: Ruby-Anne Fenning

This edition edited by Ratu Mataira and Teresa McIntyre

Printed in Malaysia via Pearson Malaysia (CTP-VVP)

A division of Pearson New Zealand Ltd

To the Teacher

There is a very good philosophy behind the new *Mathematics and Statistics Curriculum*. The aim of *Pearson Maths* is to bridge the gap between that document and classroom practice. The series emphasises real situations for using and applying mathematics.

Books 2a and 2b

Each book covers Number and Algebra, Geometry and Measurement, and Statistics.

Two major features of these books are the mini projects and the challenges.

Mini projects

These are open-ended mathematical applications. Teachers need to be able to stand back and behave as facilitators rather than controllers. Children need to be allowed to make mistakes; trial and error is a recognised problem-solving strategy. Likewise the ability to communicate in mathematics is important and the mini projects allow for a variety of ways of communicating. They allow the children to apply their mathematical vocabulary, signs and symbols.

These are an added motivation for generally, but by no means exclusively, the more able students. Some children always continue to surprise me!

The teacher is the most important factor in a child's learning. It is how a teacher makes use of published material that will encourage or discourage a child.

The *Teachers' Guides* are the centre of this series. They provide a framework and developmental structure to the teaching of mathematics. Each unit specifies particular Achievement Objectives taken from the Mathemathics and Statistics Curriculum. Each chapter has specific learning outcomes. They provide the teacher with some guidance on how to go about teaching specific objectives. The Guides may give suggestions on how to introduce a concept or provide ideas on how to extend or give further practice. A copy of each pupil's page is included in the *Teachers' Guide* as an aid to planning specific activities.

The teacher must control the programme; the programme should *not* control the teacher.

Contents

Mini Projects ?

Hello, I'm Charlotte Wilkinson. I live in Rotorua, with my husband, two daughters and two cats. I help teachers develop exciting Maths programmes in their schools.

Working with Numbers up to 20

You should know your number facts to 10, the teens numbers as 10 + and all the doubles from 1 + 1 to 10 + 10

How many number facts to 20 do you 'just know' or can work out very quickly using what you know?

$9 + 6 = 10 + 5$ $7 + 8 = 7 + 7 + 1$

Work with a friend and see who can get the answer quickest. Explain to your friend how you know the answer.

1 $9 + 4 = \boxed{}$ **2** $6 + 5 = \boxed{}$

3 $7 + 9 = \boxed{}$ **4** $8 + 6 = \boxed{}$

5 $7 + 5 = \boxed{}$ **6** $7 + 8 + 3 = \boxed{}$

7 $3 + 2 + 14 = \boxed{}$ **8** $5 + 11 + 4 = \boxed{}$

9 $4 + 7 + 2 = \boxed{}$ **10** $6 + 5 + 3 = \boxed{}$

Use your facts to 10 and your 10 + knowledge to subtract quickly.

13 − 7 = 13 − 3 − 4

This is easy because I know 13 = 10 + 3, I know 7 = 3 + 4 and I know 4 + 6 = 10

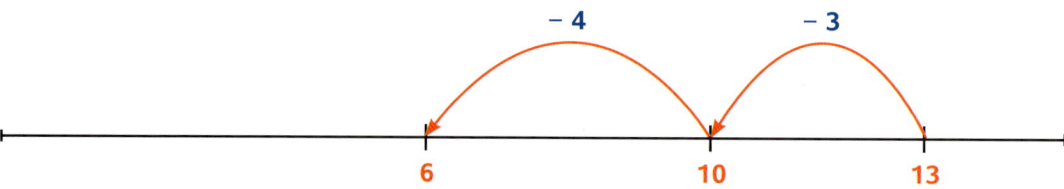

1 15 − 7 = ☐   **2** 12 − 5 = ☐

3 13 − 6 = ☐   **4** 14 − 8 = ☐

5 17 − 8 = ☐

Work with a friend and see who can get the answer the quickest. Explain to your friend how you know the answer.

6 12 − 6 = ☐   **7** 15 − 9 = ☐

8 14 − 7 = ☐   **9** 18 − 9 = ☐

10 13 − 9 = ☐

Can you remember how to subtract 9 using − 10 and + 1
Does knowing your doubles help with subtraction?

Story Problems

1 Mr Patara drives 14km to work.
Last week his car broke down after
he had travelled 11km.
How far did he have to walk to get to work?

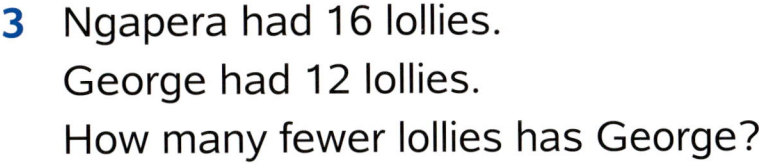

2 Amy gave out 6 party invitations on Monday.
She gave out 8 more invitations on Tuesday.
How many people has she invited to her party?

3 Ngapera had 16 lollies.
George had 12 lollies.
How many fewer lollies has George?

4 There were 8 children in the swimming pool.
4 girls and 6 boys jumped into the pool.
How many children are in the pool?

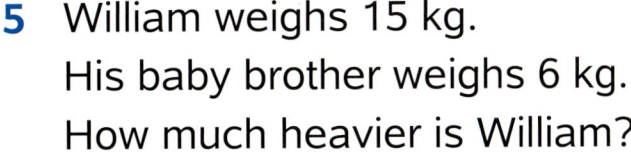

5 William weighs 15 kg.
His baby brother weighs 6 kg.
How much heavier is William?

6 Nigel is reading a book with 20 pages.
He read 6 pages before lunch and
7 pages after lunch.
How many pages has he read?
How many more pages has he to read to finish the book?

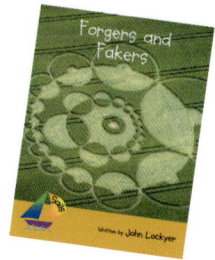

Balancing Equations

Can you help Levi cross the river?
He can only step on stones that have an equal value.

19 – 3	5 + 9	20 – 5	5 + 11	20 – 7	7 + 8
19 – 5	7 + 7	9 + 6	18 – 2	19 – 2	8 + 6
6 + 8	3 × 5	4 + 11	2 × 8	7 + 9	13 + 2
2 × 7	8 + 7	20 – 6	9 + 8	20 – 4	8 + 8

Start

Record Levi's journey as:
8 + 8 = 20 – 4 = ☐

Challenge

Can you find two other equal pathways to cross the river starting from a different stone?

Balance these equations.

5 + 8

6 + 7

1 5 + 7 = 20 − ☐

2 6 × 3 = 2 + ☐

3 4 + ☐ = 18 − 4

4 2 × ☐ = 8 + 8

5 3 + 15 = ☐ × 2

6 20 − 8 = ☐ + 6

7 19 − 5 = ☐ + 5

8 ☐ + 6 = 8 + 11

9 ☐ × 5 = 10 + 10

10 16 + 4 = 8 + ☐ + 9

Can you make these equations balance?
Try to complete each one in at least two
different ways.

11 5 + ☐ = 15 − ☐

12 6 + ☐ = 2 + ☐ + ☐

13 2 × ☐ = ☐ + 6

14 20 − ☐ = 5 × ☐

Using 'less than' and 'greater than'

| < is less than | = is equal to | > is greater than |

We can balance equations like this.

$9 + 6 = 8 + 7$

But what if the equations do not balance?

5 + 2 is less than 3 + 9
$5 + 2 < 3 + 9$

3 + 9 is greater than 5 + 2
$3 + 9 > 5 + 2$

Use the correct sign to complete these equations.

1 4 + 3 ☐ 7 + 5   **2** 12 + 6 ☐ 3 × 5

3 20 − 5 ☐ 8 + 6   **4** 2 × 7 ☐ 11 + 6

5 19 − 5 ☐ 4 + 8   **6** 12 − 3 ☐ 3 × 3

7 8 + 7 ☐ 9 + 7   **8** 18 − 6 ☐ 2 × 8

9 11 + 9 ☐ 7 + 12   **10** 3 × 6 ☐ 2 × 9

Is it True or False?

1   3 + 13 = 5 × 3   2   6 + 9 > 4 + 8

3   7 + 4 < 20 − 9   4   2 × 4 = 13 − 6

5   8 + 12 < 3 × 6   6   4 × 4 < 6 + 7

7   13 + 7 > 6 + 6 + 6   8   9 × 2 = 20 − 3

9   17 − 5 < 3 × 4   10 6 + 8 > 4 + 9

Who has less money?
John has $6 in his money box.
His mum gave him $10.
Keith had $20 and he spent $12.

6 + 10 > 20 − 12   Keith has less money.

Who Has Less Money?

Write out the mathematical equation.

11 Evie has $10 from her mum and $5 from her nan.
     Dana had $2 in her money box and she found $12.

12 Hayden had $19. He spent $8.
     Joshua had $5 and his dad gave him $5.

13 Moana had $18 and she spent $9.
     Awanui had $20 and he spent $10.

CHAPTER 2

Addition with 2 Digits

 Rounding Numbers

> **Rounding to the nearest 10 number.**
>
> **Numbers ending in 1, 2, 3, 4 round down.**
> **Numbers ending in 5, 6, 7, 8, 9 round up.**
> **23 rounds down to 20   47 rounds up to 50**

Round these numbers to the nearest 10.

1 61	**2** 79	**3** 84	**4** 27	**5** 35
6 42	**7** 96	**8** 18	**9** 3	**10** 55

> **Estimating will tell you if your answer is reasonable.**
> 57 + 32   **Rounding:**   60 + 30
>   **Estimate:**   90

Estimate the answers to these additions.

11 33 + 26   **12** 56 + 14   **13** 23 + 31

14 65 + 13   **15** 81 + 15   **16** 47 + 47

17 62 + 28   **18** 52 + 25

Working Mentally

Work with a friend.

Find the answer to a question, then discuss with your friend how you arrived at the answer.

1 34 + 9   **2** 21 + 63   **3** 7 + 24

4 52 + 12   **5** 35 + 15   **6** 64 + 3

7 Jessie ate 16 lollies on Saturday
and 21 lollies on Sunday.
How many lollies did he eat?

8 Kelly built a tower with 23 yellow
bricks and 35 blue bricks.
How many bricks did she use?

9 Ngaire had $25 in the bank and her
Mum gave her $20.
How much money does she have?

10 Arwen weighs 27kg.
Her friend Nora is 5kg heavier.
How heavy is Nora?

Did you and your friend use
the same method all the time?

Before working out a calculation, estimate the answer.
(You do not need to write down the estimate)

Calculate
48 + 36

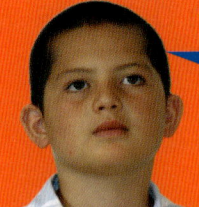

Estimate
50 + 40 = 90

How could you calculate? Use standard partitioning.
(You need to know your facts to 20.)
48 + 36
40 + 30 = 70
8 + 6 = 14
70 + 14 = 84
Is the answer reasonable? Yes, it is close to my estimate.
Or;
Using the next ten (You need to know your facts to 10.)
48 + 30 = 78
78 + 6 = 78 + 2 + 4
78 + 2 + 4 = 84

Work with a friend and talk about how you are working these additions out.

1 57 + 28 = ☐   **2** 67 + 24 = ☐   **3** 36 + 37 = ☐

4 25 + 47 = ☐   **5** 76 + 18 = ☐   **6** 53 + 38 = ☐

7 65 + 27 = ☐   **8** 44 + 48 = ☐

Another way of calculating is using compensation.

48 + 36

50 + 34

+ 2

48 + 36 = 50 + 34

− 2

Use a strategy to work out the following additions.

Discuss with a friend which strategy you have used.

Can you use more than one strategy for each question?

1 37 + 48 = ☐   **2** 69 + 18 = ☐   **3** 26 + 39 = ☐

4 24 + 26 = ☐   **5** 56 + 28 = ☐   **6** 43 + 37 = ☐

7 75 + 17 = ☐   **8** 48 + 48 = ☐

 **Story Problems**

1 Tipene was doing a weekend bike ride. One Saturday she cycled 24km and on Sunday she cycled 17km.
How far has she ridden?

2 Mum drove her car at 49km per hour. Dad was driving his car 26km per hour faster than Mum. How fast was Dad driving?

3 It is 28km from my house to Tina's house. It is another 28km from Tina's house to Peter's house. How far is it from my house to Peter's house?

4 3 bus loads of tourists arrived in Rotorua. On one coach there were 38 people, on the second coach there were 26 people and on the third coach there were 29 people. How many people arrived in Rotorua?

5 Megan has $56. Her nan gave her $25. How much money does she have?

 **Using Addition**

Look at this addition wall.
Can you see how it is built up?

Copy and complete these addition walls.

1

2

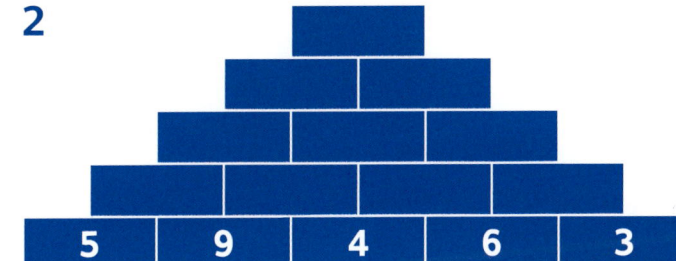

3

Challenge

Arrange the numbers 4, 5, 6, 7, 8 along the bottom of the wall in different orders. How many different totals can you get at the top of the wall?

Number Squares

1

+	34	68
29		
17		

2

+	47	28
46		
38		

3

+	36	24	18
38			
19			
56			

4

+	39	57
42		
27		

Challenge

Make up a number square yourself. Totals must be less than 100.

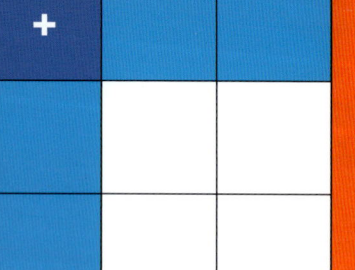

14

CHAPTER 3

Subtraction with 2 Digits

Before working out a calculation, estimate the answer. (You do not need to write down the estimate.)

$63 - 37$

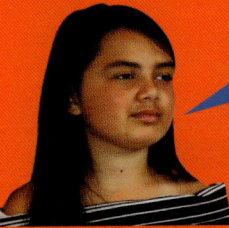

$60 - 40 = 20$

You can subtract by taking away using tens numbers. (You need to know your facts to 10.)

$63 - 30 = 33$

$33 - 7 = 33 - 3 - 4$

$30 - 4 = 26$

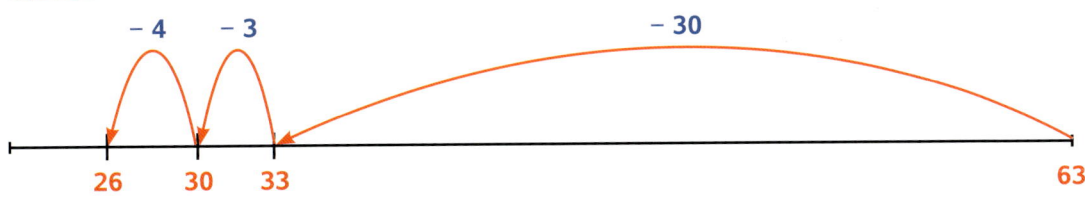

Draw a number line for each question in your book and show how you have worked out these subtractions.

1. $57 - 28 = \boxed{}$
2. $62 - 37 = \boxed{}$
3. $85 - 28 = \boxed{}$
4. $71 - 46 = \boxed{}$
5. $93 - 57 = \boxed{}$
6. $74 - 28 = \boxed{}$
7. $83 - 55 = \boxed{}$
8. $61 - 17 = \boxed{}$
9. $82 - 45 = \boxed{}$

You can subtract by using the difference between the numbers. (You need to know your facts to 10.) Make the number you are subtracting a tens number but keep the difference between the two numbers the same.

63 − 37

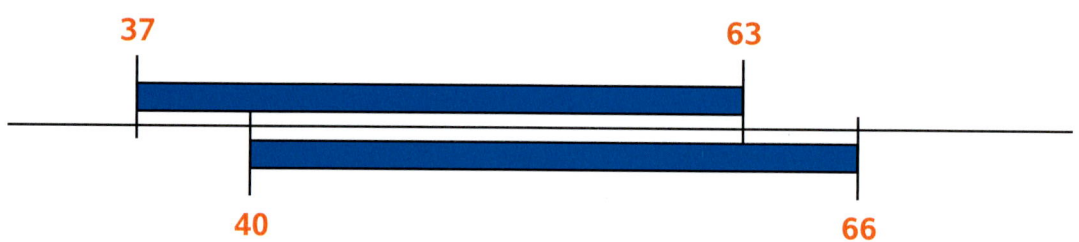

$63 - 37 = 66 - 40$

$66 - 40 = 26$

Use the difference between numbers to work out these subtractions. Draw a number line if you find it helpful.

1 77 − 38 = ☐   **2** 63 − 47 = ☐   **3** 55 − 28 = ☐

4 71 − 59 = ☐   **5** 83 − 37 = ☐   **6** 94 − 28 = ☐

7 73 − 55 = ☐   **8** 62 − 17 = ☐   **9** 84 − 46 = ☐

A Game to Practise Subtraction

Players take turns to choose 2 star numbers and find the difference between them.

If the difference is on the grid, cover the number with a counter.

The winner is the person who gets 4 in a row, horizontally, vertically or diagonally.

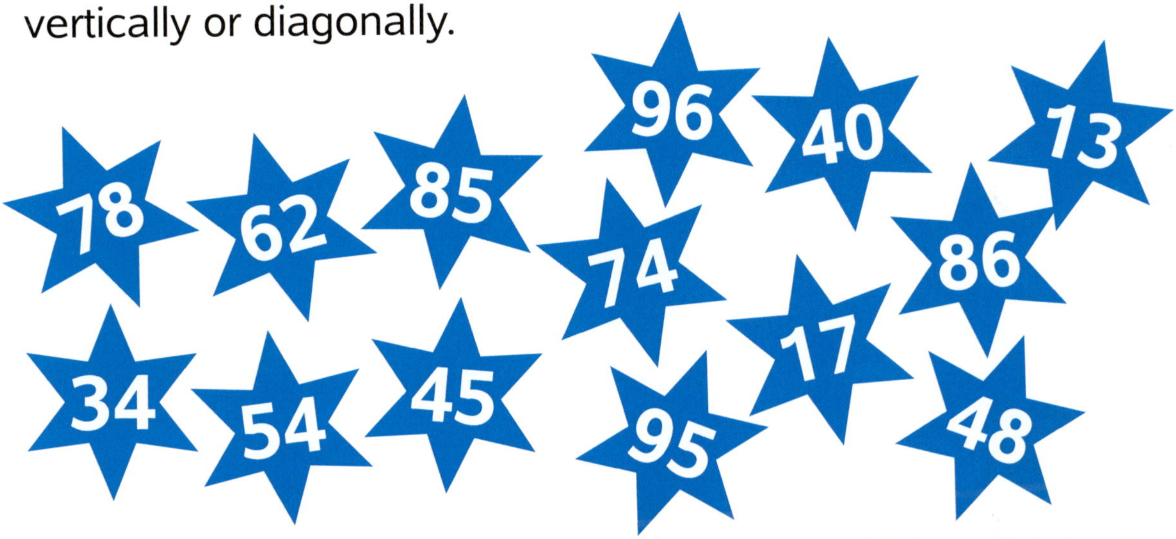

96 40 13

78 62 85 74 86

34 54 45 17 48

95

16	41	28	12	26	40	47
30	48	17	33	15	10	31
50	21	42	49	37	23	39
24	34	52	18	29	14	45
44	13	36	43	22	19	38
20	51	25	32	11	46	27

 **Story Problems**

Find the answers to these problems.

1 A pair of shoes cost $73 but they were $25 off in the sale.
What was the sale price of the shoes?

2 It's 83km from Rotorua to Cambridge.
After 44km we stopped for petrol.
How much further have we to go?

3 My dad weighs 92kg.
My mum is 26kg lighter.
How heavy is my mum?

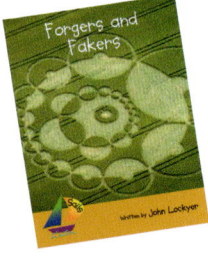

4 Tama Toa has to read 24 pages of his book for homework. He was on page 38.
What page will he finish on?

5 An aeroplane can carry 86 passengers. If 59 seats are booked, how many more people could book a flight?

Challenge

Keep a diary to find out where and when you use addition and subtraction outside the maths lesson.

Missing Bricks

Find the missing numbers on the addition walls.
You will need to use some subtraction.

1

		80		
	42			
	23		19	
12	11	8		
4		3	5	6

2

	77		
		33	
19		18	
11	8		11
	3	2	

3

36			
	20	27	
7		11	
2		4	9

Challenge

Make an addition wall
which totals 82.

82

Disco Time

Four classes are holding a disco.
There are 31 children in each class but some children
cannot go to the disco.

Class	Not going to disco
1	6 children
2	8 children
3	9 children
4	7 children

1 How many children are going to the disco altogether?

These items were left over from the last disco.
27 packets of chips
36 cans of drink
45 bars of chocolate

2 How many of each item will they need to buy to have enough for everyone going to the disco?

3 Chips can only be bought in bags of 12 packets. How many bags will they need to buy?

4 Bottles of drink are sold in trays of 12. How many trays will they need to buy?

5 Chocolate is sold in boxes of 15. How many boxes of chocolate will they need to buy?

6 If everybody at the disco has a packet of chips, a bottle of drink and a bar of chocolate, how many of each item will be left over for the next disco?

CHAPTER 4

Numbers to 999

 What is the Number After 99?

Nine is the largest digit you can have in a column, so we have to start a new column called hundreds. The next number is one hundred, written as 100.

Put ten bags of ten beans into a larger bag.
How many beans in the large bag?
How many 10s make 100?

hundreds	tens	ones

Using bags of beans, make these numbers.

1 123   **2** 106   **3** 140

4 64   **5** 102

6 What does the zero represent in each of the numbers?

7 When do you not need to use a zero?

Words and Digits

Write these numbers in figures.

1 Four hundred and thirty six.
2 One hundred and seventeen.
3 Five hundred and sixty eight.
4 Two hundred and fifty.
5 Nine hundred and two.
6 Seven hundred and forty-five.
7 Six hundred and twelve.
8 Three hundred and seven.

six hundred

6 2 1

twenty   one

Write these numbers in words.

9 731   10 403
11 626   12 370
13 806   14 513
15 128   16 244

Challenge

In how many places can you find 3-figure numbers?

Expanding Numbers

572	=	500	+	70	+	2	

Expand these numbers.

1 351   **2** 583   **3** 657

4 436   **5** 122   **6** 630

7 242   **8** 708   **9** 318

10 864   **11** 950   **12** 203

Put the following numbers in order from smallest to largest.

13 272, 328, 156

14 563, 421, 807

15 151, 582, 376, 253

16 298, 542, 241, 423

17 195, 488, 172, 453, 129

18 286, 354, 126, 477, 235, 408

1 2 3 4 5 6 7 8 . . . .

3 Digit Numbers

1 Write all the numbers you can
using the numerals 3, 5 and 7.
Here are two numbers: 357, 537

2 Write your numbers again in order
starting with the smallest.

What is the place value of each orange numeral in the
numbers below?

3 574   **4** 758   **5** 129

6 683   **7** 443   **8** 910

9 721   **10** 388   **11** 267

12 503   **13** 428   **14** 543

Challenge

**How many 3-figure numbers
can you write using the
numerals 6, 0, 2?**

One More One Less

Write the number that is one more than the given number.

1 234   **2** 469   **3** 399

4 289   **5** 899   **6** 579

7 740   **8** 600   **9** 499

Complete the following equations:

10 299 + 1 = ☐   **11** 500 + 1 = ☐   **12** 799 + 1 = ☐

13 499 + 1 = ☐

Write the number that is one less than the given number.

14 600   **15** 210   **16** 500

17 560   **18** 780   **19** 900

20 450   **21** 940   **22** 200

Complete the following equations:

23 200 − 1 = ☐   **24** 420 − 1 = ☐   **25** 704 − 1 = ☐

 **10 More 10 Less**

Write the number that is 10 more than the given number.

1 236   **2** 674   **3** 501

4 396   **5** 217   **6** 591

7 198   **8** 95   **9** 794

Complete the following equations:

10 268 + 10 = ☐   **11** 594 + 10 = ☐   **12** 603 + 10 = ☐

13 495 + 10 = ☐

Write the number that is 10 less than the given number.

14 538   **15** 461   **16** 780

17 708   **18** 631   **19** 307

20 609   **21** 400   **22** 108

Complete the following equations:

23 679 − 10 = ☐   **24** 308 − 10 = ☐   **25** 102 − 10 = ☐

Challenge

Write the number that is one more than 999.
Write the number that is 10 more than 999.

27

Continue these number sequences.

1	348	448	548	____	____	____
2	589	489	389	____	____	____
3	260	270	280	____	____	____
4	558	568	578	____	____	____
5	650	640	630	____	____	____
6	844	834	824	____	____	____

Game

You will need a partner and 0 – 9 digit cards.

Lay the cards face down on the table.
Turn over three cards each.

If you can make the largest number
with your three cards score 2 points.

If you can make the smallest number
with your three cards score 2 points.

Whoever makes the number closest
to 500 scores 2 points.

Replace your three cards, mix them up and play again.
First person to score a total of 10 points is the winner.

 **How Many Tens?**

2	3	6

This picture represents 236.

How many bags of ten beans are there in the picture altogether?

In each hundred bag are 10 small bags.
10 small bags + 10 small bags + 3 bags = 23 bags of ten.
There are 23 tens in the number 236.

How many tens are in each of these numbers?
Make the numbers using beans if you find it helpful.

1 348 **2** 184 **3** 429

4 258 **5** 703 **6** 569

7 921 **8** 32 **9** 637

Explain how you came to your answer.

Addition and Subtraction with Money

In New Zealand the bank issues these notes and coins.

Notes

Coins

What is the least number of notes and coins you would use to make each of the following amounts? Show which notes and coins you would use, e.g. $12 = $10 + $2

1 $14	**2** $36	**3** $57
4 $83	**5** $72	**6** $25
7 80c	**8** 30c	**9** 90c
10 $6.30	**11** $13.60	
12 $27.80	**13** $42.60	
14 $63.40	**15** $76.70	

Challenge

What values can you make using 2 notes and 2 coins?

 **How Much Money?**

Write the price tag for each item.

1 A guitar costs
$50 + $20 + $20
+ $5 + $2 + 50c

2 A soccer ball costs
$20 + $5 + $1 + 50c
+ 20c + 20c

3 A dartboard costs
$20 + $10 + $5 + $2
+ $1 + 20c

4 A bunch of flowers costs
$10 + $2 + 50c + 10c

Going Shopping

$5.30

$10.50

$2.50 each

$24.80

How much?

1 The sunglasses and a comb.
How much change from $10.00?

2 The box of chocolates and two balloons.
How much change from $20.00?

3 The teddy and the monkey.
How much change from $70.00?

4 Four pencils and three lollipops.
How much change from $10.00?

5 The dinosaur and two pencils.
How much change from $20.00?

$1.50 each

50c each

$1.50

$35.50

$16.50

6 The teddy, a pair of sunglasses and two lollipops.
How much change from $40.00?

7 Two combs, a box of chocolates and a teddy.
How much change from $50.00?

8 The monkey, four balloons and two lollipops.
How much change from $50.00?

Challenge

How would you spend $50.00?

At the Café

Jason and Rina were helping their auntie in her café during the school holidays. Their auntie asked them to keep a record of what their customers ordered on one Saturday.

Jason's Customers	
Burgers	THL THL THL THL THL //
Sausage & chips	THL THL THL ////
Chicken nuggets & chips	THL THL THL //
Fish & chips	THL THL //
Milkshake	THL THL THL THL THL THL //
Muffin	THL ///\
Cake	THL THL THL ///

Rina's Customers	
Burgers	THL THL THL THL ////
Sausage & chips	THL THL THL THL THL /
Chicken nuggets & chips	THL THL THL
Fish & chips	THL THL THL ///
Milkshake	THL THL THL THL THL ///
Muffin	THL THL //
Cake	THL /

Find the total number of each item sold:

1 Burgers
2 Sausage & chips
3 Chicken nuggets & chips
4 Fish & chips
5 Milkshake
6 Cake

7 Rahera ordered:
   • fish & chips   • a muffin   • a milkshake.
   a How much was the meal?
   b Rahera paid with the exact money. What notes and coins could have been given to Jason?

c If Rahera paid with coins, what is the least number of coins he would have given to Jason and what were they?

8 Mark and Hayley went into the café.
Mark ordered: • a burger • a muffin • a milkshake.
Hayley ordered: • chicken nuggets & chips • a cake • a milkshake.

a How much was Mark's meal?

b How much was Hayley's meal?

c Mark paid for both meals with a $20 note. How much change will he have?

9 You have a $10 note. Choose a meal from the menu that you would like.

a How much will it cost?

b How much change will you have?

c What notes and coins could you have given to pay the exact cost?

Challenge

Use a calculator to work out how much money was taken at the café this Saturday. Who took more money – Jason or Rina?

CHAPTER 6

Multiplication By 3 and By 9

 ## Skip Counting in 3s

Continue the following sequences:

1 0, 3, 6, 9, _____ , _____ , _____ , _____

2 15, 18, 21, _____ , _____ , _____ , _____

3 15, 12, _____ , _____ , _____ , _____

4 30, 27, _____ , _____ , _____ , _____

Count in threes:

5 How many flowers?   6 x 3 = _____

6 How many fish?   5 x 3 = _____

7 How many cookies?   3 x 3 = _____

Using the Two Times Table

> **5 groups of 3 is the same as 5 groups of 2 and 5 groups of 1.**
>
> **5 x 3 = (5 x 2) + (5 x 1)**
>
> **5 x 3 = 10 + 5**
>
> **5 x 3 = 15**

1 Use counters to make 7 groups of 3.

Make each group of 3 into a group of 2 and a group of 1.

Put all the groups of 2 together: 7 x 2 = _____

Put all the groups of 1 together: 7 x 1 = _____

Add your answers together: _____ + _____ = _____

Complete the following questions:

2 6 x 3 = (6 x 2) + (6 x 1)

6 x 3 = _____ + _____

6 x 3 = _____

3 8 x 3 = _____ + _____

8 x 3 = _____ + _____

8 x 3 = _____

 **Word Problems**

1 Class Four had 7 tables in their classroom.
On each table were 3 library books.
How many library books altogether?

2 On Monday 9 children each brought
$3 to school for the disco. How much
money was collected on Monday?

3 Sarah read three pages of her reading
book every evening for five days.
How many pages has she read?

4 William played for 3 hours every day on
his computer for 6 days. How many hours
has he spent playing on his computer?

5 Mark bought 8 packets of gum.
In each packet were 3 sticks of gum.
How many sticks of gum does he have altogether?

Challenge

**Make up some more multiply by three
stories for your friends to solve.**

Learning the Nine Times Table

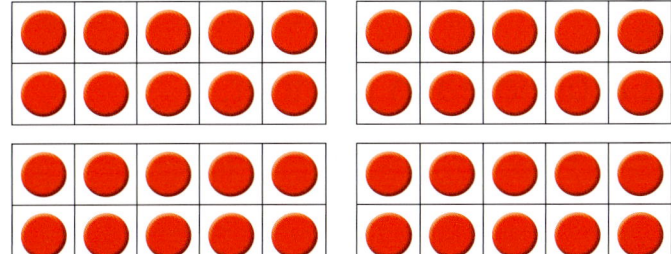

4 x 10 = 40

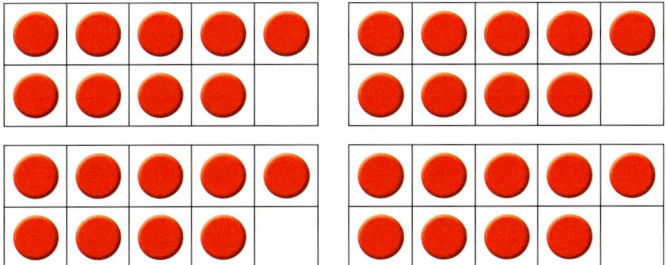

4 x 9 = (4 x 10) − (4 x 1)

4 x 9 = 40 − 4

4 x 9 = 36

Complete the following:

1 3 x 9 = (3 x 10) − (3 x 1)

3 x 9 = _____ − _____

3 x 9 = _____

2 7 x 9 = (7 x 10) − (7 x 1)

7 x 9 = _____ − _____

7 x 9 = _____

3 6 x 9 = _____ − _____

6 x 9 = _____ − _____

6 x 9 = _____

4 9 x 9 = _____ − _____

9 x 9 = _____ − _____

9 x 9 = _____

5 5 x 9 = _____ − _____

5 x 9 = _____ − _____

5 x 9 = _____

6 8 x 9 = _____ − _____

8 x 9 = _____ − _____

8 x 9 = _____

 **A Closer Look**

You need a hundred square.
Count in threes, put a circle around each number.
Count in sixes, put a square around each number.

1	2	③	4	5	⬜⑥	7	8	⑨	10
11	⬜⑫	13	14	⑮	16	17	⬜⑱	19	20
21	22	23	24	25	26	27	28	29	30
31	32	33	34	35	36	37	38	39	40
41	42	43	44	45	46	47	48	49	50
51	52	53	54	55	56	57	58	59	60
61	62	63	64	65	66	67	68	69	70
71	72	73	74	75	76	77	78	79	80
81	82	83	84	85	86	87	88	89	90
91	92	93	94	95	96	97	98	99	100

- Can you see a pattern?
  Can you explain a rule for this pattern?
- On your hundred square, count in nines, put a triangle around each number.
  What do you notice?
- Could you make a general statement about the numbers in the three, six and nine times tables?

Challenge

Try making the 12 × table on the 100 square as well.

 **Look Again**

To find these patterns you need to look at the 'ones' digit in each number.

Counting in threes:
3, 6, 9, 12, 15, 18, 21, 24, 27, 30, 33, 36.

- Draw a circle and label it 0–9.
- Start at 3, draw a line to 6, then a line to 9, then a line to 2 (2 is the 'one' digit in the number 12).
- Continue drawing lines until the pattern is complete.

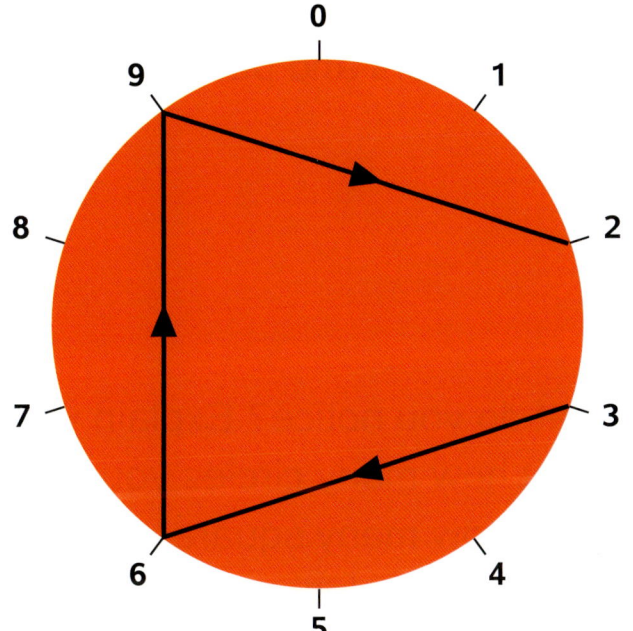

Will the pattern be the same for counting in sixes? Try it.
Can you predict the pattern for the nines? Were you right?

Challenge

Find out which tables share the same patterns.

You will need a hundred square.
Count in twos and put a circle around every 2nd number.
Count in fours and put a square around every 4th number.

1	②	3	④	5	⑥	7	⑧	9	⑩
11	⑫	13	14	15	16	17	18	19	20
21	22	23	24	25	26	27	28	29	30

What do you notice? Explain your pattern in words.
Count how many circles you have drawn up to number 24.
Count how many squares you have drawn up to number 24.
Number of circles = _____
Number of squares = _____
Count how many circles up to number 48.
Count how many squares up to number 48.
Number of circles = _____
Number of squares = _____
Can you see a relationship between the number of circles
and the number of squares? What is it?
Check to see if this is true using any number with a square
drawn round it.

Now you will need a large piece of squared paper (at least 40 squares) and two different coloured pencils.

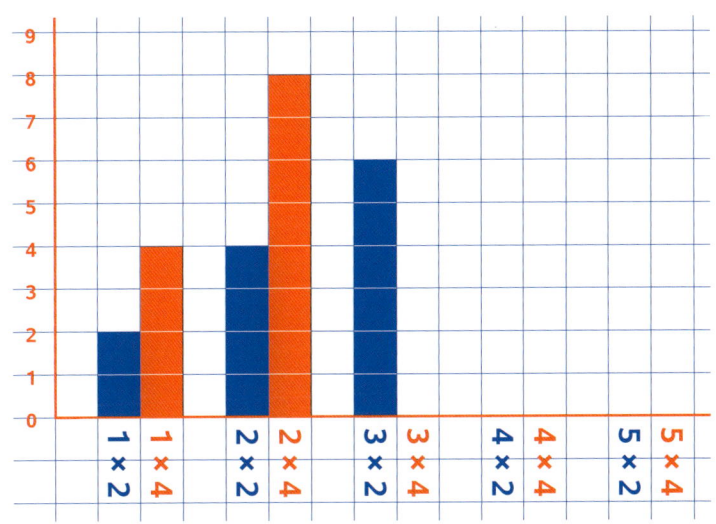

From your picture complete the following questions.

1 1 x 2 = 2
    1 x 4 = 4

2 2 x 2 = _____
    2 x 4 = _____

3 3 x 2 = _____
    3 x 4 = _____

4 4 x 2 = _____
    4 x 4 = _____

5 5 x 2 = _____
    5 x 4 = _____

6 6 x 2 = _____
    6 x 4 = _____

7 7 x 2 = _____
    7 x 4 = _____

8 8 x 2 = _____
    8 x 4 = _____

9 9 x 2 = _____
    9 x 4 = _____

10 10 x 2 = _____
    10 x 4 = _____

What is the relationship between the two times and the four times tables?

The four times table is _____ the two times table.

Twos and Fours

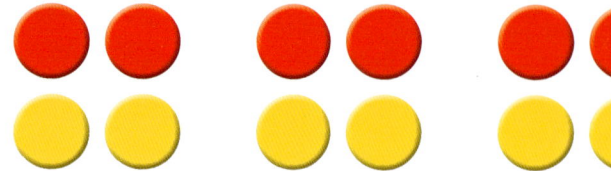

3 x 4 = (3 x 2) + (3 x 2)

3 x 4 = 6 + 6

3 x 4 = 12

1 Use counters to make 6 groups of 4.
Make each group of 4 into groups of two.

6 x 4 = (6 x 2) + (6 x 2)

6 x 4 = _____ + _____

6 x 4 = _____

2 7 x 4 = (7 x 2) + (7 x 2)

7 x 4 = _____ + _____

7 x 4 = _____

When I multiply by 4
I just double the number
then double it again.

3 8 x 4 = _____ + _____

8 x 4 = _____ + _____

8 x 4 = _____

 **Story Problems**

1 Charlotte went fishing on 4 separate days last month. She caught 4 fish each time. How many fish did she catch last month?

2 Eric was working in the garden. He noticed 4 caterpillars on each of his 8 cabbage plants. How many caterpillars altogether?

3 How many paws altogether are there on 6 cats?

4 Four bars of chocolate in a bag are being sold as a supermarket special. Mum bought 3 bags of specials. How many bars of chocolate did she buy?

5 On the school trip four children can go in each car. 9 cars went on the trip. How many children went on the trip?

Multiplication Facts

How well are you learning your multiplication facts?
Write the answers only for each column

A

4 x 2 = ☐
6 x 5 = ☐
7 x 2 = ☐
4 x 10 = ☐
2 x 3 = ☐
5 x 9 = ☐
3 x 4 = ☐
6 x 3 = ☐
8 x 2 = ☐
3 x 9 = ☐

B

5 x 5 = ☐
4 x 9 = ☐
7 x 3 = ☐
8 x 5 = ☐
2 x 9 = ☐
4 x 3 = ☐
8 x 4 = ☐
3 x 10 = ☐
6 x 2 = ☐
3 x 3 = ☐

C

7 x 10 = ☐
8 x 3 = ☐
6 x 2 = ☐
5 x 4 = ☐
7 x 5 = ☐
4 x 4 = ☐
9 x 9 = ☐
5 x 10 = ☐
6 x 9 = ☐
9 x 2 = ☐

Challenge

Time yourself.
Keep a record of your time.
Do them again, can you beat your time.

Story Problems

1 4 children each had 9 lollies.
How many lollies altogether?

2 There are 5 trees in the garden and 4 birds
in each tree. How many birds altogether?

3 There were 3 tuatara in each of 5 cages at
the zoo. How many tuatara altogether?

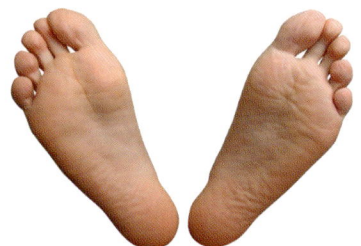

4 How many feet on 8 children?

5 How many toes on 6 children?

6 Jenny has 3 money boxes.
In each money box she had $9.
How much money does she
have altogether?

Challenge

Make up some more
multiplication stories and give
them to your friends to solve.
Put all your stories into a booklet.

CHAPTER 8

Sharing or Grouping

Do you share your lollies with your friends? In maths we must share equally ... to be fair!

Give your answers to the next seven questions in words and pictures.

1 Mako had 12 lollies. He shared them with Ngaru and Devon. How many lollies will they have each?

Mako	**Ngaru**	**Devon**

(You can use counters instead of lollies.)

They will have _____ lollies each.

2 10 kittens are shared between 5 baskets. How many kittens are in each basket?

3 20 dollars is shared between 4 children. How much money has each child?

4 12 muffins are shared between 6 children. How many muffins does each child have?

5 24 books are shared between 2 classes. How many books does each class have?

6 16 marbles are shared between 4 boys. How many marbles does each boy have?

7 18 lollies are shared between 3 girls. How many lollies does each have?

Challenge

Take 12 counters. Share them between 2, 3, 4 and 6 people. Can you always share them equally? Can you find another good sharing number?

 **Grouping**

Find 8 cubes.
How many groups of 2 can you make?

8 cubes makes 4 groups of 2.

Give your answers in words and pictures.

1 Find 15 cubes.

How many groups of 5 can you make?

2 Find 10 cubes.

How many groups of 2 can you make?

3 Find 18 cubes.

How many groups of 3 can you make?

4 Find 20 cubes.

How many groups of 4 can you make?

Challenge

You will need 24 matchsticks.
How many triangles can you make?
How many squares can you make?
How many hexagons can you make?
How many octagons can you make?

Grouping as Repeated Subtraction

An egg carton holds 6 eggs.
How many cartons will be needed to put
30 eggs in the bowl?

Show your answers as repeated subtraction.

1 A bottle holds 10 mL.

How many bottles can you fill with 50 mL of water?

50 – ☐ – ☐ – ☐ – ☐ – ☐ = 0

I can fill _____ bottles.

2 Each towel needs 2 pegs.

How many towels can I hang up with 16 pegs?

3 Each bag holds 5 kg of potatoes.

How many bags will I fill if I have 35 kg of potatoes?

4 A crate holds 9 bottles.

How many crates do I need to hold 27 bottles?

Use a calculator to solve these problems.
Press **3** **0** **–** **6** **=** **=** **=** **=** **=**
What do you need to press for questions 1–4?

Sharing or Grouping

Find the answer.

1 If there are 18 balloons, how many children can have 2 balloons each?

2 There are 16 legs in the paddock. How many horses are there?

3 There are 6 frogs shared equally between 2 ponds.
How many frogs are in each pond?

4 I sewed 6 buttons on each shirt. How many shirts can I make with 30 buttons?

5 Share 20 biscuits between 5 children. How many biscuits will they have each?

6 The teacher had 12 stickers. How many stickers would 6 children get each?

7 Amanda had 24 marbles.
She shared them with 3 of her friends.
How many marbles will each child have?

8 There are 3 fish in each bowl.
How many bowls will there be
if there are 21 fish?

9 Dad had $18.00. He shared it
between my two brothers and me.
How much money did we each get?

10 Every biscuit contains 12 raisins.
How many biscuits can be made
with 48 raisins?

11 Mr Paora had 36 carrots.
He put 6 in each bag.
How many bags did he use?

Challenge

Make up some
sharing and
grouping stories
for your friends.

12 A bucket holds
5 litres. How
many buckets
will it take to
fill up a 40-litre
paddling pool?

At the Beach

Eastland School is going on a trip to the beach.
Can you help them find the answers to these questions?

1 How many cars are needed, if each car can take 4 children?

Class	Number of children	Number of cars
A1	36	
A2	32	
A3	28	

2 How many children are going altogether?

3 How many cars are going altogether?

Someone muddled up the lunches.
This is what they had.

Class	Sandwiches	Apples	Biscuits	Drinks
A1	53	17	36	21
A2	32	51	43	16
A3	11	28	17	59

There should be a sandwich, an apple, a biscuit and a drink for each child.

4 Help the classes sort out how many of each item they need to give away and to which class or classes.

After lunch there was a sandcastle competition.
40 children took part in the competition.
They worked in groups of 8.

5 How many sandcastles were built?

6 To decorate their castles, Mrs Collins has collected 45 shells, 30 stones and 15 pieces of seaweed. She shared them equally between the groups. How many shells, stones and pieces of seaweed did each group get?

7 How many children did not build sandcastles? These children worked in groups of 8 to look in rock pools.

8 How many groups were looking in rock pools?

9 Each group found 4 starfish, 2 crabs and 3 shrimps. How many starfish, crabs and shrimps were found?

Challenge

Use a calculator to work out this problem. 30 children wanted strawberry ice-cream at $1.10 each. 24 children wanted hokey pokey ice-cream at $1.20 each. The rest of the children had lime ice-cream at $1.00 each. How much was the ice-cream bill?

CHAPTER 9

Rounding Numbers

The tens numbers from 1 to 100 are

0 10 20 30 40 50 60 70 80 90 100

Write the tens numbers from:

1 100 to 200   **2** 400 to 500

3 300 to 400   **4** 800 to 900

Half of 100 is 50.

What number is halfway between:

5 100 and 200   **6** 300 and 400

7 600 and 700   **8** 800 and 900

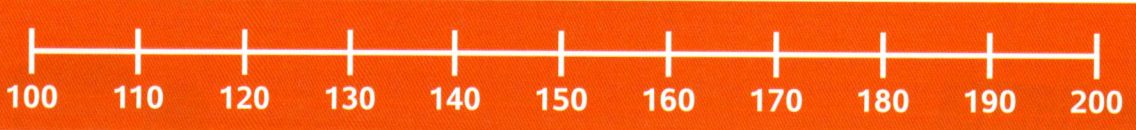

100   110   120   130   140   150   160   170   180   190   200

100 or 200?

9 120 is nearer to _____.   **10** 180 is nearer to _____.

11 140 is nearer to _____.   **12** 160 is nearer to _____.

The middle number is always said to be nearer the higher number – so 150 is nearer to 200.

Rounding to the Nearest 100

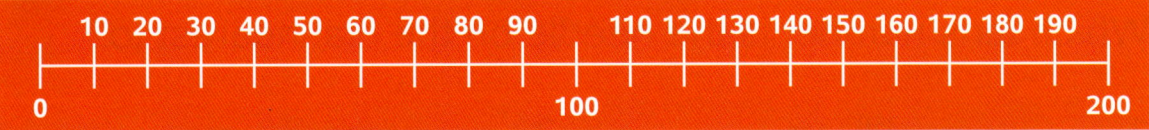

Round these numbers to the nearest hundreds number.

1 60	**2** 160	**3** 260	**4** 360
5 130	**6** 320	**7** 150	**8** 250
9 380	**10** 290	**11** 110	**12** 30

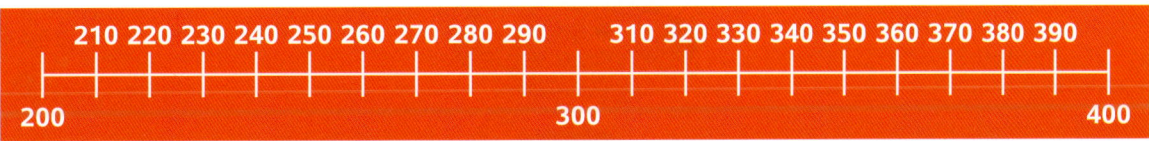

Round these numbers to the nearest hundreds number.

13 420	**14** 910	**15** 750	**16** 460
17 820	**18** 530	**19** 730	**20** 860
21 640	**22** 970	**23** 540	**24** 650

Rounding to the Nearest Ten

Which tens number is the needle on the dial nearest to?

1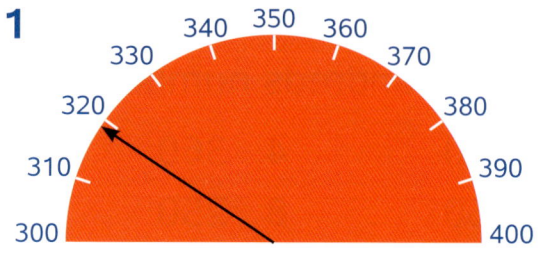

2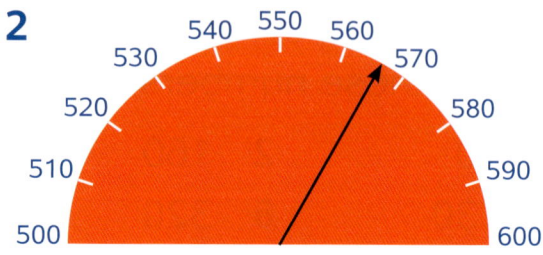

3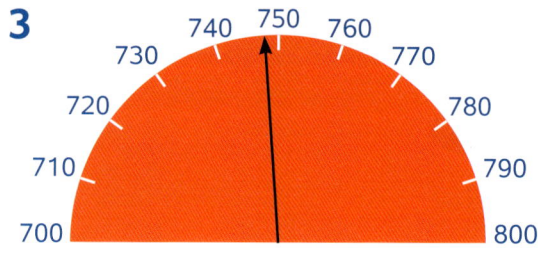

4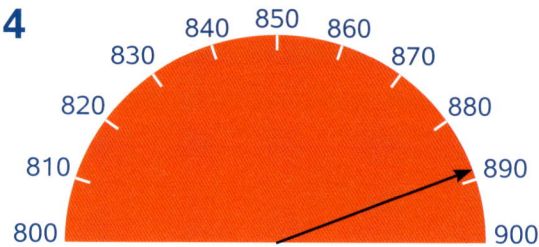

5 Which hundreds number is the needle on each dial nearest to?

6 What number do you think the needle on each dial is pointing to?

Rounding numbers helps you to make an estimated answer.
Complete the table.

	Number	Round to nearest 10	Round to nearest 100
	176	180	200
1	332		
2	569		
3	421		
4	855		
5	739		
6	203		
7	684		
8	914		
9	38		
10	535		

Estimate the answers to the nearest hundred.

159 + 323 = $\longrightarrow$ 200 + 300 = 500

11 368 + 296 = $\longrightarrow$

12 571 + 214 = $\longrightarrow$

13 617 + 134 = $\longrightarrow$

Challenge

Estimate the answers to the nearest 10. Use a calculator to find the actual answer. Which gives you the best estimate – rounding to the nearest hundred or rounding to the nearest ten?

CHAPTER 10

Addition with 3 Digits

 ## Using Hundreds

345 + 199 =

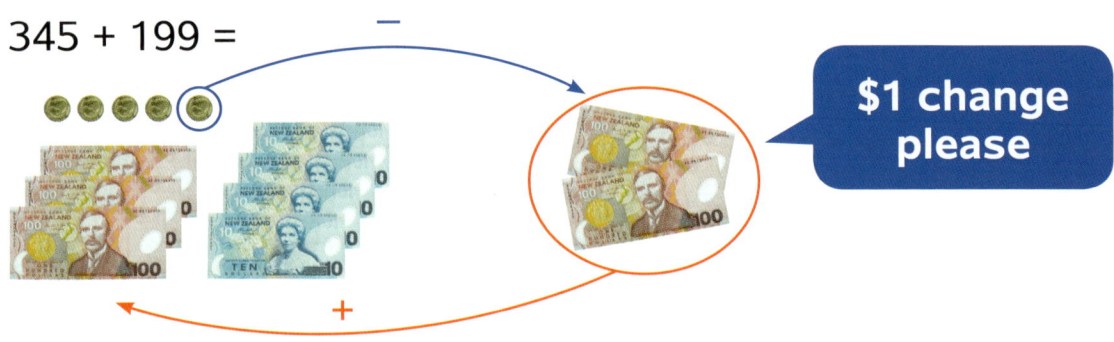

$1 change please

345 + 199 = 345 + 200 − 1

545 − 1 = 544

Using only $100 notes from the bank and your $1 coins, act out these additions with a partner and record the answers.

1 $365 + $199 =   2 $376 + $399 =

3 $723 + $298 =   4 $552 + $198 =

5 $466 + $299 =   6 $538 + $397 =

7 $634 + $498 =   8 $745 + $297 =

9 $645 + $197 =   10 $445 + $399 =

Challenge

$599 + $235 =

$498 + $385 =

$799 + $145 =

Making Tidy Numbers

436 + 296 =

  **+**

=

+4

436 + 296 = 432 + 300

432 + 300 = 732

Use tidy numbers to solve these equations.

1 367 + 194 = 361 + 200
361 + 200 =

2 648 + 395 =

3 526 + 296 =

+3

4 428 + 347 = 425 + 350
425 + 350 =

5 554 + 238 =

6 348 + 145 =

+3

7 427 + 364 = 430 + 361
430 + 361 =

8 368 + 227 =

9 549 + 233 =

Challenge

Using tidy numbers show how many different ways you could solve this equation.
448 + 448 =

Using Standard Partitioning

This means pull the numbers apart into hundreds, tens and ones – then add the hundreds, add the tens and add the ones, then add all the parts together again.

458 + 367 =
400 + 50 + 8 + 300 + 60 + 7
400 + 300 = 700
50 + 60 = 110
8 + 7 = 15
700 + 110 + 15 = 825

Use standard partitioning to solve these equations.

1   385 + 247 =
2   247 + 486 =
3   538 + 275 =
4   634 + 328 =
5   538 + 277 =
6   366 + 444 =

Choose two different strategies to solve each of these equations.
Show the strategies you have used and explain them to a friend.

7   539 + 248 =
8   483 + 377 =
9   258 + 242 =
10 676 + 197 =

Story Problems

Choose a stratergy to solve each of these problems.

1 Beth was doing some cooking. The recipe said 245mL of milk and 255mL of water was needed. How much liquid does Beth need?

2 Erueti was up to page 186 in his book. He read 72 pages at the weekend. What page is he on now?

3 Ranui drove 143km from Gisborne to Opotiki. Then he drove 157km from Opotiki to Tauranga. How far did Ranui drive?

4 Mrs Falconer was rearranging her classroom. If a desk measures 437mm, how much space does she need for 2 desks?

5 Class 4 ran all the way around the field. The sides of the field measured 193m, 207m, 248m and 287m. How far did Class 4 run?

6 A banana weighs 278g. How much do 2 bananas weigh?

Challenge

Write some addition stories of your own. Give them to a friend to solve.

Using a Calculator Accurately

Read the number marked by each arrow and use your calculator to find the total for each number line.
Your total should match the check total.

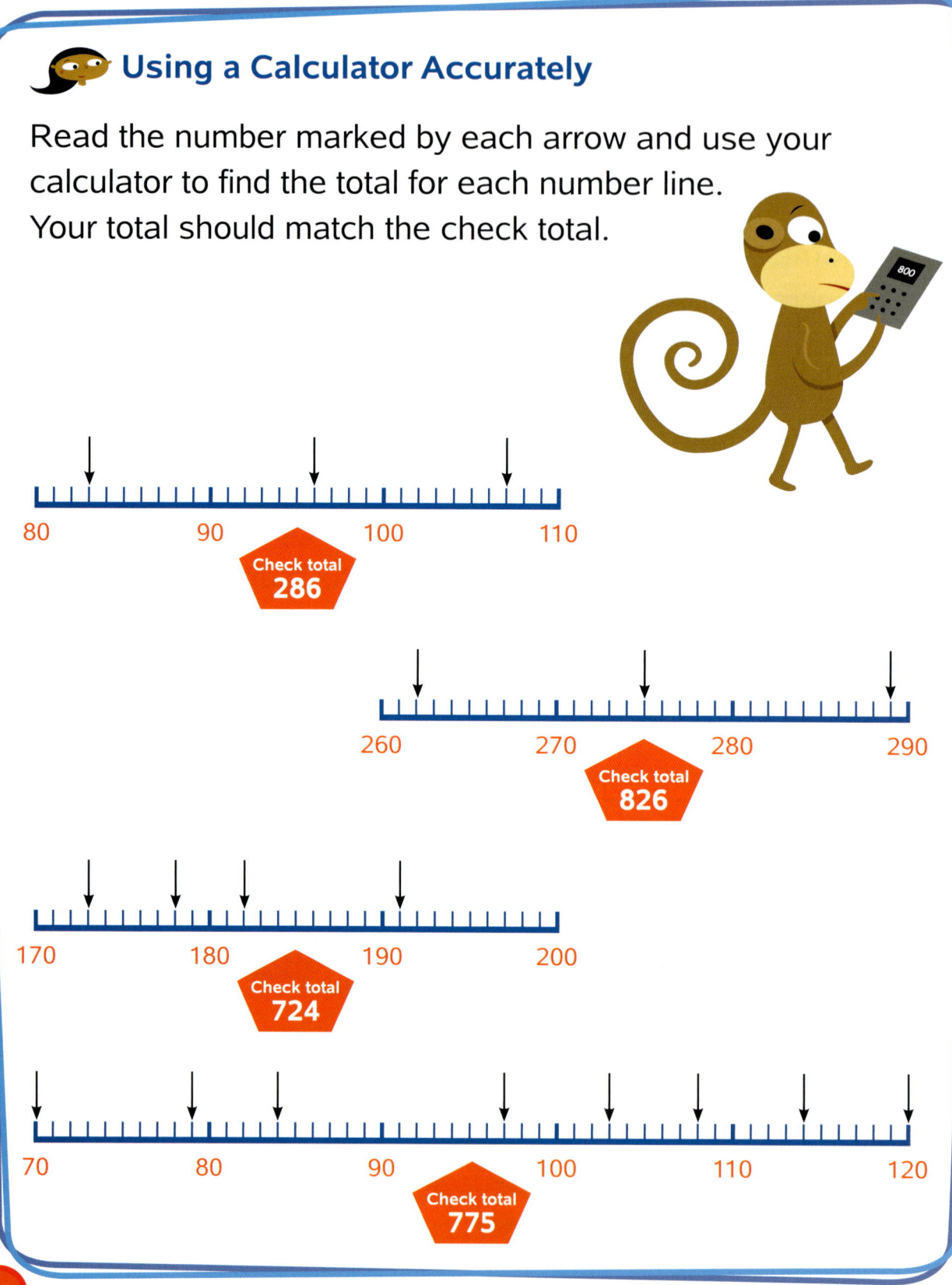

Check total
286

Check total
826

Check total
724

Check total
775

Estimations and Calculators

Copy and complete the table.

Question	Estimation	Answer on calculator
284 + 537	300 + 500 = 800	821
139 + 420	100 + 400 =	
603 + 294		
478 + 396		
539 + 187		
619 + 223		
496 + 123		
106 + 594		
447 + 365		
760 + 124		
315 + 121		

Challenge

Make a triangle jigsaw. Make 4 triangles the same as the picture. Use your calculator to work out the addition sum on each edge.

Cut out the 4 triangles and put them together to make a large triangle, so that touching sides have the same answer.

How many different ways can you do this?

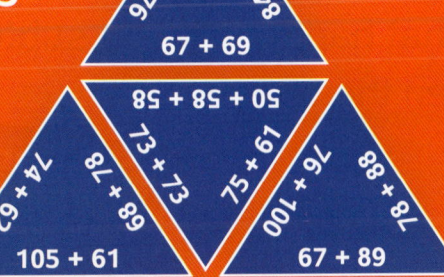

CHAPTER 11

Subtraction with 3 Digits

 Using Place Value to Subtract

568 − 235 =

> Remember: 235 = 200 + 30 + 5

Subtract hundreds, then tens, then ones:
568 − 200 = 368
368 − 30 = 338
338 − 5 = 333

Solve the following equations:

1 684 − 342 =   **2** 857 − 625 =

3 947 − 316 =   **4** 768 − 436 =

5 589 − 324 =

What happens if you subtract the ones, then the tens and then the hundreds?

What happens if you subtract the tens, then the hundreds, then the ones?

Challenge

671 − 433 =

836 − 563 =

 ## Using Hundreds

562 − 199 =

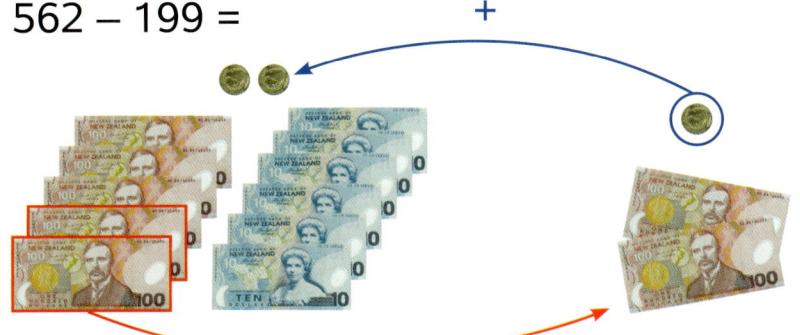

$199

Here's your change

$562 − $199 = $562 − $200 + $1

$362 + $1 = $363

Make the first number in each equation with money notes. Then, using only the $100 notes and $1 coins from the 'bank' act out these subtractions with a partner and record the answers.

1 $456 − $199 =
3 $587 − $199 =
5 $637 − $198 =
7 $864 − $498 =
9 $687 − $299 =

2 $645 − $299 =
4 $736 − $298 =
6 $386 − $197 =
8 $724 − $397 =
10 $577 − $398 =

Challenge

$500 − $296 =
$600 − $492 =
$800 − $589 =

Using Difference Between Two Numbers

Make the number you are subtracting a tidy number and keep the difference between the numbers the same.

456 − 238 = 458 − 240

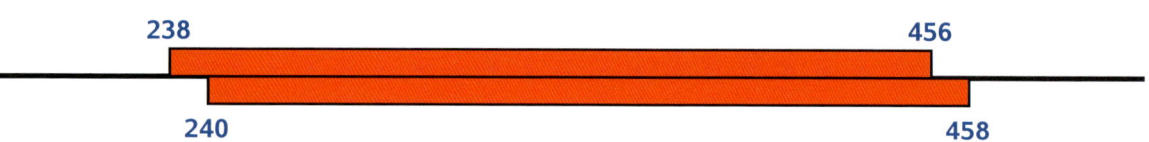

458 − 240 = 218

Use subtracting a tidy number to solve these equations.
Draw a number line if it is helpful.

1 367 − 237 =   **2** 484 − 317 =

3 845 − 516 =   **4** 767 − 438 =

5 662 − 438 =   **6** 576 − 267 =

7 368 − 138 =   **8** 782 − 548 =

Estimating Answers

Rounding to the nearest hundred:

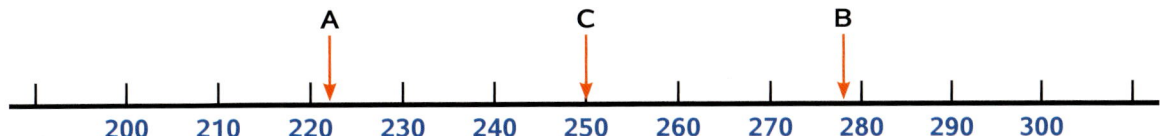

Arrow A at number 222 rounds to 200
Arrow B at number 278 rounds to 300
Arrow C at number 250 rounds to 300

Rounding is used to estimate answers.
Estimate the answers to the nearest hundred:
1 378 – 246 =
    400 – 200 =
2 568 – 120 =
3 879 – 368 =
4 735 – 432 =
5 686 – 389 =

Challenge

Estimate the answers to the nearest 10.
Use a calculator to find the actual answer.
Which gives the closest estimate – rounding to
the nearest 100 or rounding to the nearest 10?

A Subtraction Investigation

0 1 2 3 4 5 6 7 8 9

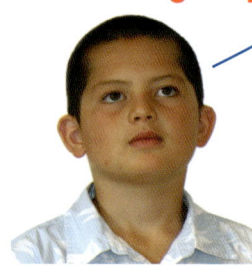

Mako chose 3 consecutive digits.
He reversed them,
then subtracted them: **432 − 234 = 198**

0 1 2 3 4 5 6 7 8 9

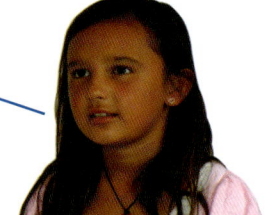

Devon chose 3 consecutive digits.
She reversed them,
then subtracted them: **876 − 678 = 198**

Now you choose 3 consecutive digits and try the same.
Try this at least 5 times.
What do you notice?

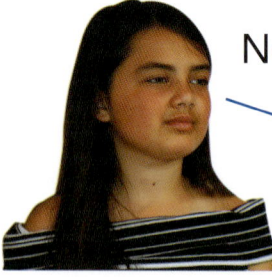

Ngaru decided to try alternate digits.

2 4 6   **642 − 246 = 396**

Try some more using 3 alternate digits.
What answers do you get?

Some of the children decided to investigate further.
They chose any three digits.

Wade chose   1, 5, 9   Horiana chose   2, 4, 8
951 − 159 =   **842 − 248 =**

Jason chose   2, 3, 5   Emily chose   2, 8, 9
532 − 235 =   **982 − 289 =**

Courtney chose   0, 8, 9   George chose   1, 5, 6
980 − 89 =   **651 − 156 =**

Work out the subtractions for these children.
Try some more of your own.
How many different answers can you get?
Look at your answers. Do you notice a pattern?

Challenge

Investigate what happens when you use
a   **4 consecutive numbers**
b   **5 consecutive numbers.**

Fractions

1   If a circle is folded into 2 equal parts, each part is called a _____ .

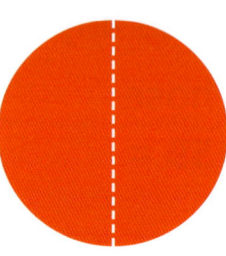

2   If a circle is folded into 4 parts, each part is called a _____ .

3   1 whole = _____ halves = _____ quarters.

This strip has been folded into 3 equal parts. Each part is called a third.

One-third is written $\frac{1}{3}$

4   1 whole = _____ thirds.

This strip has been folded into 5 equal parts. Each part is called a fifth.

One-fifth is written $\frac{1}{5}$

5   1 whole = _____ fifths.

Use cuisinare rods to complete the following activities.

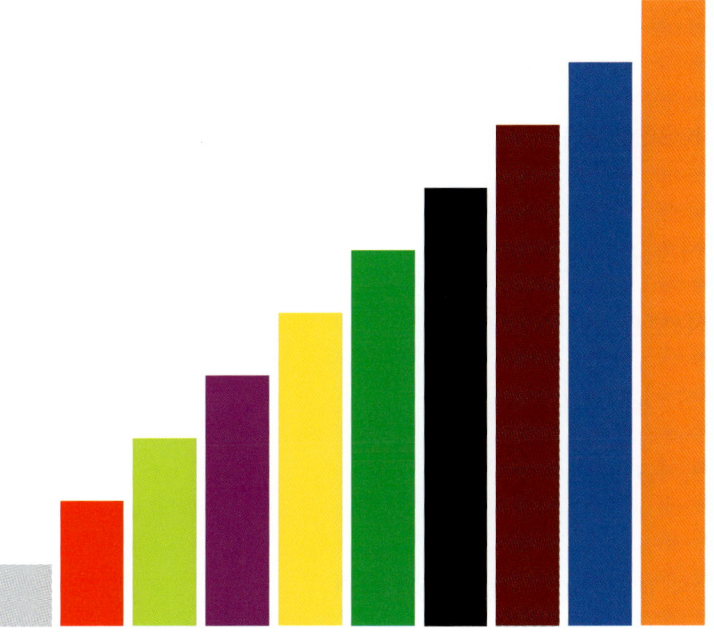

Find the orange rod.

1   Which colour rod is $\frac{1}{5}$ of the orange rod?

2   Which colour rod is $\frac{1}{2}$ of the orange rod?

Find the blue rod.

3   Which colour rod is $\frac{1}{3}$ of the blue rod?

4   The pink rod is $\frac{1}{2}$ of which colour rod?

5   The red rod is $\frac{1}{4}$ of which colour rod?

Explain why the red rod can be a $\frac{1}{4}$ and a $\frac{1}{5}$?
What has changed?

Ordering Fractions

You will need 4 one-metre strips of paper.

Fold each strip and keep them folded with a paper clip.

Strip 1 – fold in half, label it $\frac{1}{2}$.

Strip 2 – fold in quarters, label it $\frac{1}{4}$.

Strip 3 – fold in thirds, label it $\frac{1}{3}$.

Strip 4 – fold in fifths, label it $\frac{1}{5}$.

Now place your strips in order of length.

Write the order of the fractions from smallest to largest:

_____   _____   _____   _____

Challenge

If you had the fractions $\frac{1}{12}$, $\frac{1}{6}$, $\frac{1}{9}$ and $\frac{1}{20}$: which is the largest fraction and which is the smallest fraction?
Explain why.

Which is bigger?

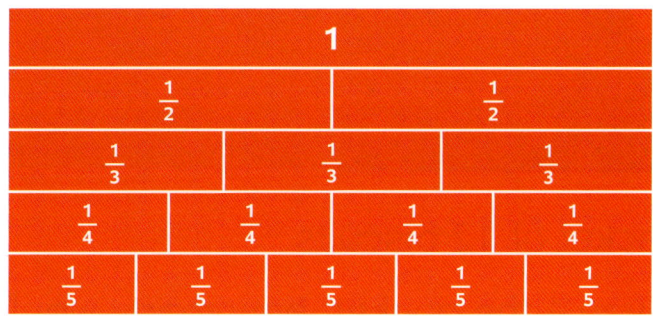

Use the table to compare the fractions.
Use the signs > greater than or < less than to complete these equations.

1   $\frac{1}{2}$ ☐ $\frac{1}{3}$ 2 $\frac{1}{5}$ ☐ $\frac{1}{4}$ 3 $\frac{1}{3}$ ☐ $\frac{1}{4}$

4   $\frac{1}{4}$ ☐ $\frac{1}{2}$ 5 $\frac{1}{5}$ ☐ $\frac{1}{3}$ 6 $\frac{1}{2}$ ☐ $\frac{1}{4}$

7   $\frac{1}{2}$ ☐ $\frac{1}{5}$ 8 $\frac{1}{3}$ ☐ $\frac{1}{2}$ 9 $\frac{1}{3}$ ☐ $\frac{1}{5}$

10   $\frac{1}{5}$ ☐ $\frac{1}{2}$ 11 $\frac{1}{4}$ ☐ $\frac{1}{5}$ 12 $\frac{1}{4}$ ☐ $\frac{1}{3}$

Challenge

What fraction of each shape is not coloured?

a    b    c   d

CHAPTER 13

Fractions of Numbers

John had a packet of 12 biscuits.

1   If he gave you $\frac{1}{2}$ the packet, how many would you have?

2   If he gave you $\frac{1}{3}$ of the packet, how many would you have?

3   If he gave you $\frac{1}{4}$ of the packet, how many would you have?

4   Which fraction will give you the most biscuits? $\frac{1}{2}$, $\frac{1}{3}$ or $\frac{1}{4}$?

Jenny had a packet of 8 biscuits.

5   If she gave you half her biscuits, how many would you have?

$\frac{1}{2}$ of Jenny's biscuits is the same as $\frac{1}{3}$ of John's biscuits. Does $\frac{1}{2} = \frac{1}{3}$?

Of course not. It depends on the size of the whole – in this case the number of biscuits in the whole packet.

When working with fractions you need to remember the size of the whole unit.

Use counters to help you solve these fraction problems.

1 There are 24 children in the class.
Half are boys and half are girls.
How many boys are in the class?
How many girls are in the class?

2 Nigel caught 9 fish but $\frac{1}{3}$ were too
small so he threw them back.
How many fish did he throw back?

3 Jenny invited 12 children to her party.
$\frac{1}{4}$ of them were boys.
How many boys came to her party?

4 There were 25 biscuits in the packet.
$\frac{1}{5}$ of them were broken.
How many biscuits were broken?

5 Jesse had $18.00.
He spent $\frac{1}{3}$ of his money.
How much has he spent?

Challenge

Write story problems for $\frac{1}{2}$ of 16,
$\frac{1}{3}$ of 15, $\frac{1}{4}$ of 20 and $\frac{1}{5}$ of 10.

Island Designer

Penny Pirate designed a new island on which to bury her treasure.

This is what her island looked like.

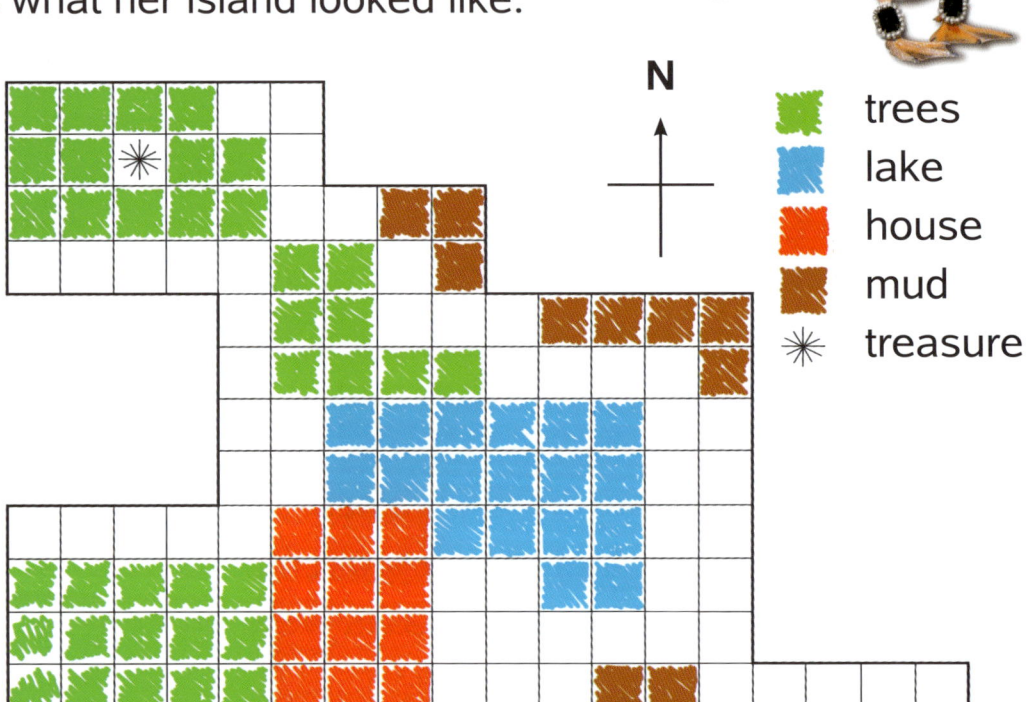

N

trees
lake
house
mud
✳ treasure

What is the area of Penny's island?
(Count the number of squares.)
She planted trees on $\frac{1}{4}$ of her island.
She dug a lake which took up $\frac{1}{8}$ of the island.
She built a house which took up $\frac{1}{12}$ of the island.
$\frac{1}{6}$ of the island was unusable because of boiling mud pools.

1. How many squares are used for tree planting?
2. How many squares are used for boiling mud?
3. What is the area of the lake?
4. What is the area of Penny's house?

5. Design another island for Penny Pirate.
   It must have the same area.
   (Use the same number of squares.)

   $\frac{1}{8}$ of your island is boiling mud.
   $\frac{1}{12}$ is taken up by a volcano.
   $\frac{1}{12}$ is used for a house.
   $\frac{1}{3}$ is covered in trees.

6. Choose a spot to bury the treasure.
7. Write a list of directions for Penny
   to find the treasure from her house.

CHAPTER 14

Division

'Divide by' means < **shared between or in groups of** > **and is represented by the symbol ÷**

12 lollies shared between 4 children.

12 ÷ 4 = ☐ lollies each.

12 children in groups of 4

12 ÷ 4 = ☐ groups.

Sharing Lollies

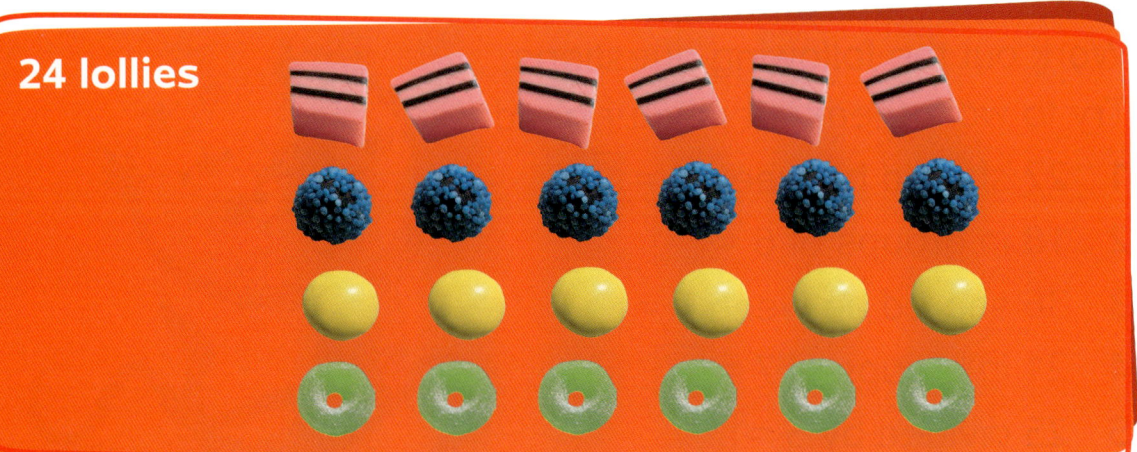

24 lollies

1 24 ÷ 4 = ☐   **2** 24 ÷ 6 = ☐

3 24 ÷ 3 = ☐   **4** 24 ÷ 2 = ☐

5 24 ÷ 8 = ☐   **6** 24 ÷ 12 = ☐

Grouping Apples

36 apples

1 36 ÷ 4 = ☐   **2** 36 ÷ 9 = ☐

3 36 ÷ 6 = ☐   **4** 36 ÷ 3 = ☐

5 36 ÷ 2 = ☐   **6** 36 ÷ 12 = ☐

More Division

Work out the following questions.
Try to work them out in your head.

1 27 shared between 3 = ☐

2 18 in groups of 6 = ☐

3 36 shared between 4 = ☐

4 21 in groups of 7 = ☐

5 25 divided by 5 = ☐

6 32 divided by 8 = ☐

7 16 divided by 4 = ☐

8 15 divided by 3 = ☐

9 40 ÷ 10 = ☐   **10** 30 ÷ 5 = ☐   **11** 20 ÷ 4 = ☐

12 9 ÷ 3 = ☐   **13** 24 ÷ 4 = ☐   **14** 35 ÷ 7 = ☐

15 18 ÷ 3 = ☐   **16** 12 ÷ 6 = ☐   **17** 28 ÷ 4 = ☐

18 10 ÷ 2 = ☐   **19** 42 ÷ 6 = ☐   **20** 14 ÷ 7 = ☐

Crack the Division Code

Find the names of these New Zealand cities.

2	3	4	5	6	7	8	9	10
a	c	h	i	o	r	s	t	u

Work out the answer to each division and find the right letter to spell the name of a city.

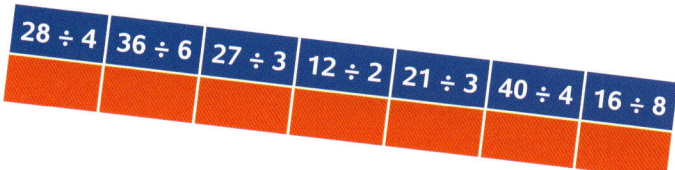

28 ÷ 4	36 ÷ 6	27 ÷ 3	12 ÷ 2	21 ÷ 3	40 ÷ 4	16 ÷ 8

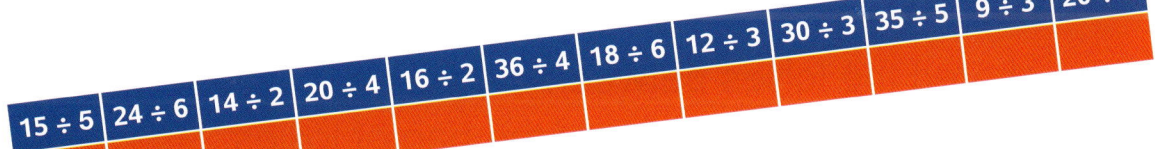

15 ÷ 5	24 ÷ 6	14 ÷ 2	20 ÷ 4	16 ÷ 2	36 ÷ 4	18 ÷ 6	12 ÷ 3	30 ÷ 3	35 ÷ 5	9 ÷ 3	20 ÷ 5

Challenge

Find these places on a map of New Zealand.

Fractions and Division

If you share an apple equally
between four you get $\frac{1}{4}$ each.

$\frac{1}{4}$ each

The bottom number (the denominator)
tells us how many equal parts there are.

Mum had a bag of 24 lollies.
If she shared the lollies between 2 children,
each child would have half the bag of lollies.

1 $\frac{1}{2}$ of 24 is $24 \div 2 =$

If she shared the lollies between 3 children,
each child would have a third of the bag of lollies.

2 $\frac{1}{3}$ of 24 is $24 \div 3 =$

If she shared the lollies between 4 children,
each child would have a quarter of the bag of lollies.

3 $\frac{1}{4}$ of 24 is $24 \div 4 =$

Find

4 $\frac{1}{3}$ of 18   **5** $\frac{1}{4}$ of 16   **6** $\frac{1}{5}$ of 30

Story Problems

Use a calculator to find the answers.

1 Sharon is reading a book with 212 pages.
She has read $\frac{1}{4}$ of the book.
How many pages has she read?

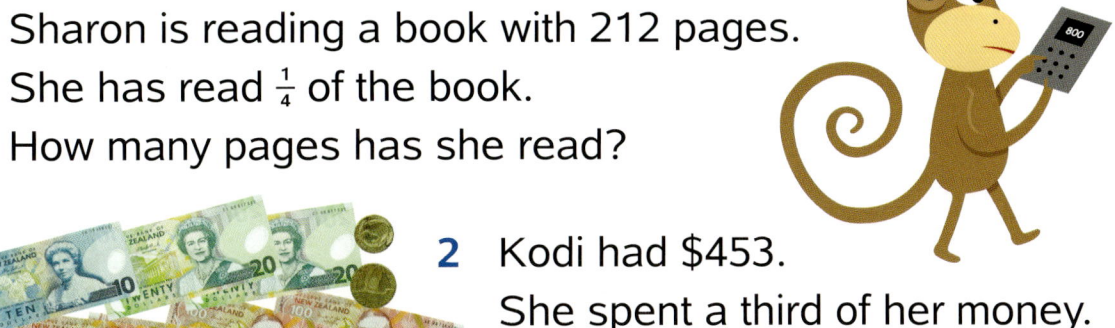

2 Kodi had $453.
She spent a third of her money.
How much has she spent?

3 Farmer Dean picked 565 apples.
$\frac{1}{5}$ of them were bad.
How many apples did he throw away?

Auckland 236 km

4 It is 236km from Rotorua to Auckland.
Paero has driven halfway.
How much further has he to go?

5 A swimming pool holds 996 litres of water.
At the moment it is $\frac{1}{3}$ full.
How much water is in the pool?

Challenge

Write story problems for:
a $\frac{1}{5}$ of 460   **b** $\frac{1}{3}$ of 372   **c** $\frac{1}{4}$ of 860

CHAPTER 15

Multiplication and Division

> 3 groups of 2 = 6   3 × 2 = 6
> 6 in groups of 2 = 3 groups   6 ÷ 2 = 3

Division is the opposite of multiplication.

1   12 in groups of 4 = _____
because _____ × 4 = 12

2   20 in groups of 5 = _____
because _____ × 5 = 20

3   16 in groups of 8 = _____
because _____ × 8 = 16

4 24 ÷ 6 = _____
because _____ × 6 = 24

5 21 ÷ 3 = _____
because _____ × 3 = 21

6 12 ÷ 2 = _____
_____ × 2 = 12

7 9 ÷ 3 = _____
_____ × 3 = 9

8 16 ÷ 4 = _____
_____ × 4 = 16

9 30 ÷ 5 = _____
_____ × 5 = 30

10 18 ÷ 6 = _____
_____ × 6 = 18

11 27 ÷ 3 = _____
_____ × 3 = 27

12 8 ÷ 2 = _____
_____ × 2 = 8

Using the Multiplication Square

The quickest way to answer division problems is to know your multiplication tables – inside out!

✕	1	2	3	4	5	6	7	8	9	10
1	1	2	3	4	5	6	7	8	9	10
2	2	4	6	8	10	12	14	16	18	20
3	3	6	9	12	15	18	21	24	27	30
4	4	8	12	16	20	24	28	32	36	40
5	5	10	15	20	25	30	35	40	45	50
6	6	12	18	24	30	36	42	48	54	60
7	7	14	21	28	35	42	49	56	63	70
8	8	16	24	32	40	48	56	64	72	80
9	9	18	27	36	45	54	63	72	81	90
10	10	20	30	40	50	60	70	80	90	100

$3 \times 5 = 15$
$5 \times 3 = 15$
$15 \div 3 = 5$
$15 \div 5 = 3$

Complete the following equations.

1 $4 \times 8 = $ _____
   $8 \times 4 = $ _____
   _____ $\div 4 = 8$
   _____ $\div 8 = 4$

2 $5 \times 6 = $ _____
   $6 \times 5 = $ _____
   _____ $\div 5 = 6$
   _____ $\div 6 = 5$

3 $3 \times $ _____ $= 27$
   _____ $\times 3 = 27$
   $27 \div 3 = $ _____
   $27 \div $ _____ $= 3$

4 $6 \times $ _____ $= 24$
   _____ $\times 6 = 24$
   $24 \div 6 = $ _____
   $24 \div $ _____ $= 6$

Multiples and Factors

4 is a factor of 20

20
4   5

20 is a multiple of 4 and a multiple of 5

4 × 5 = 20   20 ÷ 5 = 4
5 × 4 = 20   20 ÷ 4 = 5

5 is a factor of 20

Write out the multiplication and division equations from these sets of multiples and factors.

1

28
4   7

a 4 × 7 = _____
b 7 × 4 = _____
c 28 ÷ 7 = _____
d 28 ÷ 4 = _____

2

36
9   4

a 9 × _____ = _____
b 4 × _____ = _____
c 36 ÷ _____ = _____
d 36 ÷ _____ = _____

3

45
5   9

4

72
9   8

5

35
5   7

Challenge

What are all the possible factors?

12
?   ?

Multiplication and Division Problems

1 72 parents were coming to watch a show.
There is room for 8 rows of chairs at the back of the hall.
How many chairs will be in each row?

2 There are six eggs in a box.
How many eggs are in 4 boxes?

3 8 sheep all had twins.
How many lambs were there?

4 Jenny shared a packet of 18 biscuits
with three of her friends.
How many biscuits did they each get?

5 Six people went to a restaurant.
The bill came to $54.00.
They decided to all pay an equal share.
How much did they each pay?

6 Jason wears only black socks. He is
going on holiday for 7 days. How many
pairs of black socks must he pack?

7 Mr MacGregor planted 32 cabbages.
He made rows of 8 cabbages.
How many rows did he plant?

8 Todd owned 3 cars.
They all needed 4 new tyres.
How many tyres must he buy?

9 The display stand holds 5 books on each shelf.
The librarian has 3 shelves to fill.
How many books can she display?

10 The 5 children in the basketball team all
scored the same number of goals. The total
score was 35. How many did each child score?

11 The 4 runners in the relay team each ran 5km.
How long was the race?

12 Mr Griffin gave out 27 stickers.
The lucky children had 3 stickers each.
How many lucky children were there?

Challenge

**Make up some multiplication and
division stories of your own.**

Investigating Square Numbers

You will need a pot of counters.

Use counters to build squares.
Count how many counters there
are in each square.

Write out the sequence of numbers for
the number of counters in each square.

1, 4, ☐ , ☐ , ☐ , ☐ , ☐ , ☐ , ☐ , ☐ ,

Find these numbers on a hundred square.
What pattern do they make?

Write out the multiplication facts for each number.

1 = 1 × 1

4 = 2 × 2

These numbers are
called square numbers.

Look at the sequence of square numbers again.
Can you find the pattern?
What would the next number be?

Number Spells

Wilma Witch is now allowed to make bigger and better spells.

Like:

$2 \times 7 < 8 + 8$ $24 \div 8 = 7 - 4$

Help Wilma make some big spells.

What is the biggest spell you could make?

Change one of the numbers in the cauldron for a 5.
Make some new spells.
Don't forget the magic words!!

'Maths is fun!'

Work through each of these flow charts lots of times using your calculator. What do you notice?

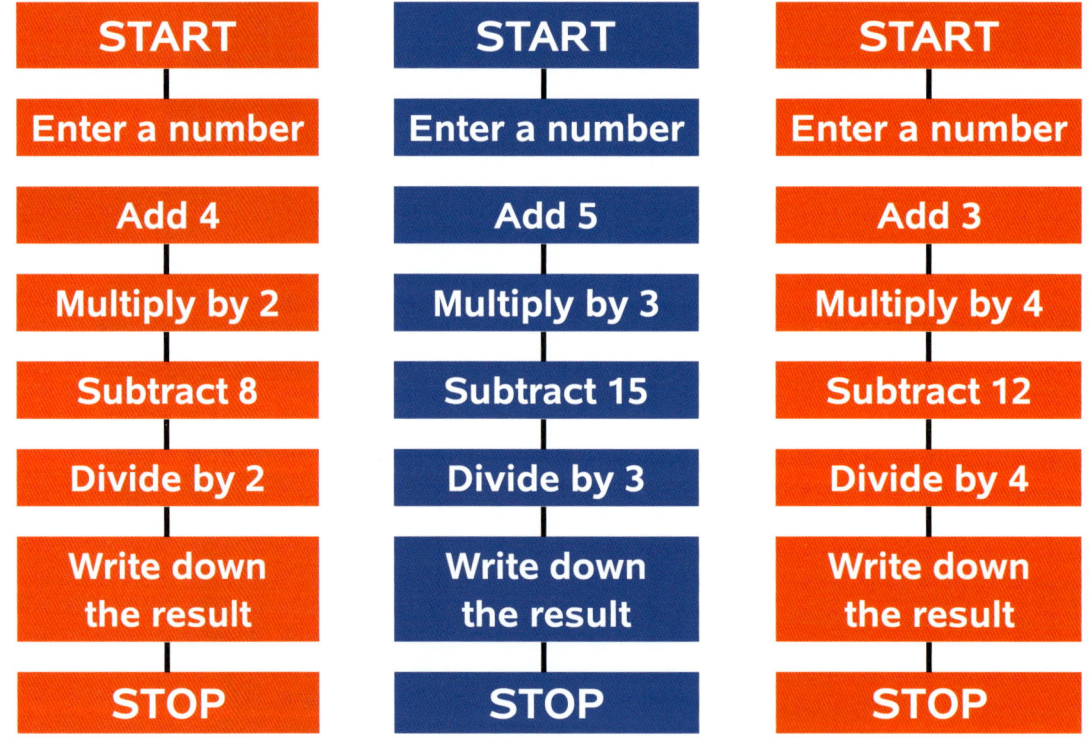

START	START	START
Enter a number	Enter a number	Enter a number
Add 4	Add 5	Add 3
Multiply by 2	Multiply by 3	Multiply by 4
Subtract 8	Subtract 15	Subtract 12
Divide by 2	Divide by 3	Divide by 4
Write down the result	Write down the result	Write down the result
STOP	STOP	STOP

Challenge

Design your own flow charts which have the same effect.

Does 0 work?

Magic Squares

In a magic square, the numbers in all horizontal, vertical and diagonal lines have the same total – the magic number.

1 In this magic square the magic number is **34**

Copy and complete the square.

In these magic squares, you have to find the magic number. **?**

	15		4
12			
	10	11	5
13	3		16

Find the magic number then copy and complete the squares.

2

1	14		12
	4		
10	5	16	
8			13

3

2	15		
16	5	10	7
11		17	
	12	3	

Triple Totals

You need:
- **two sets of 1–9 number cards**
- **paper and pencil**
- **a calculator.**

1. Shuffle the cards.
2. Place four cards on the diagram opposite.
3. Write down the three numbers you can make.
4. Use your calculator to add them together.

For example:

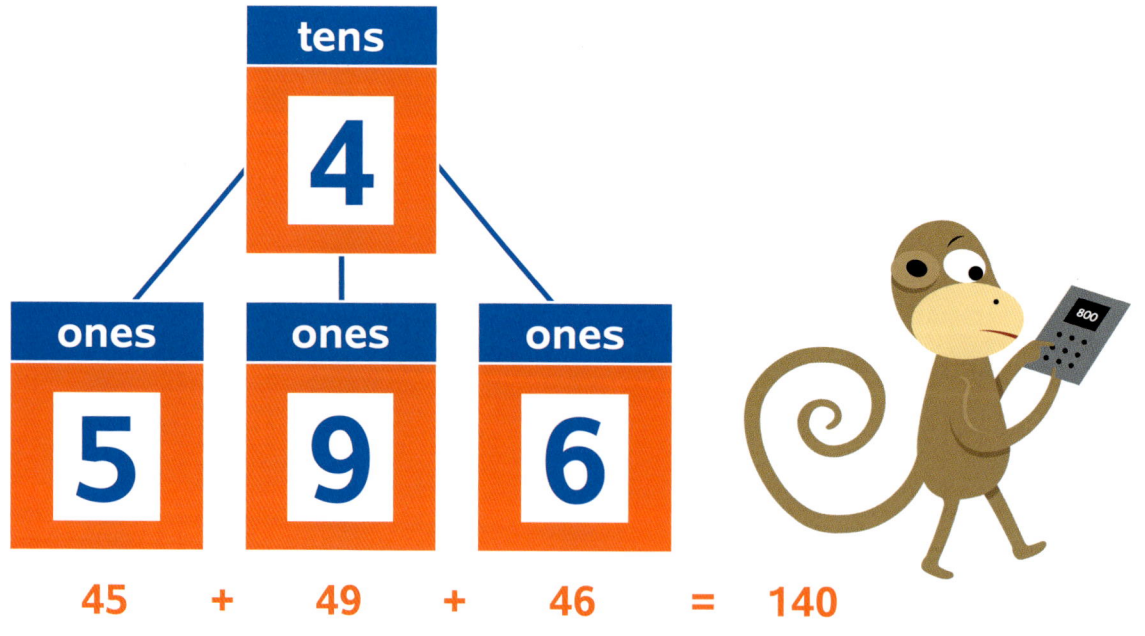

tens

4

ones **ones** **ones**

5 **9** **6**

45 + 49 + 46 = 140

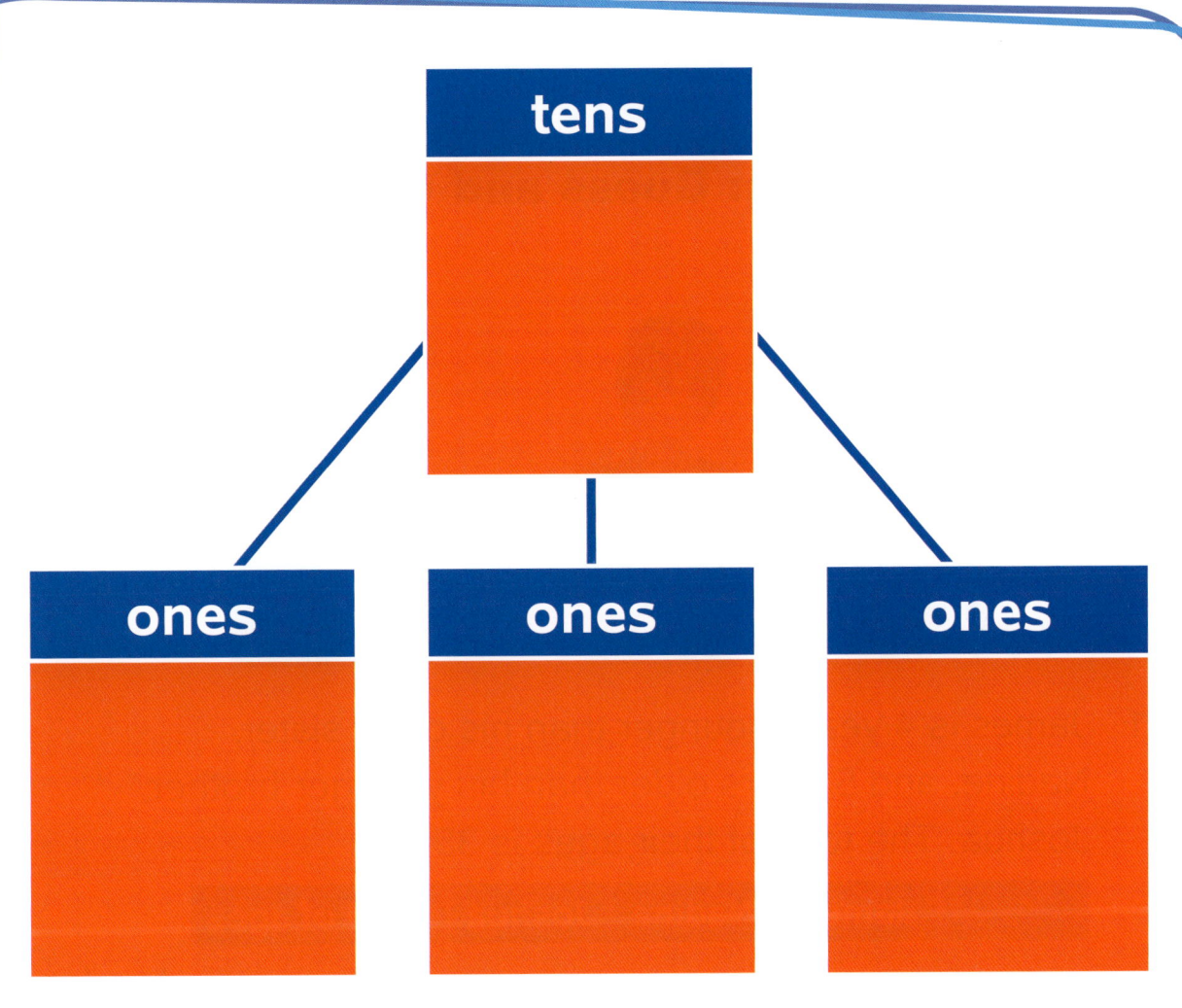

Can you get exactly 100? Or 200?
How many ways can you do this?
What is the largest total you can make?
What is the smallest total you can make?

Problem Solving: Guess and Check

1   James is 4 years younger than his older sister,
Nadine, and 5 years older than his younger brother,
Joshua. The total of their ages is 35.

	James	Nadine	Joshua	Total of ages	
Guess	10	14	5	29	too low
Guess					

2   Mrs Raki has three children: William, Eddie and Nicki.
William is twice as old as Eddie.
Nicki is 6 years older than Eddie.
When William was born, Nicki was 2 years old.
The total of their ages is 22. How old are the children?

	William	Eddie	Nicki	Total of ages
Guess				

3 Sarita, Kaylib and George collect stickers.
Kaylib has twice as many as George.
George has 15 more than Sarita.
The total number of stickers
between them is 149.
How many stickers have Sarita,
Kaylib and George?

What's the number?

4 When 32 is added to the number, the answer is the same as if you had multiplied the number by 5. What is the number?

5 When 35 is added to the number, the answer is the same as if you had multiplied the number by 6. What is the number?

6 When 15 is subtracted from the number, the answer is the same as if you had divided the number by 6. What is the number?

7 When 16 is subtracted from the number, the answer is the same as if you had divided the number by 3. What is the number?

CHAPTER 17

The Four Operations

You now know how to
- **add numbers** $8 + 2 = $ _____
- **subtract numbers** $8 - 2 = $ _____
- **multiply numbers** $8 \times 2 = $ _____
- **divide numbers** $8 \div 2 = $ _____

Which operation would you use for these problems?
State the operation used and the answer.

1 I had $25 and my mum gave me $10 more.
How much money do I have?

2 Michael is 12cm taller than his brother.
Michael is 149cm tall. How tall is his brother?

3 A table seats four children.
How many tables does Mrs
Edward need for her 28 pupils?

Challenge

Write story
problems for
each of the four
operations.

4 David has 6 bags of lollies.
Each bag contains 4 lollies.
How many lollies are there
altogether?

Opposite Operations

Addition, or adding on, is often used to solve difference-type problems.

1 Find the difference between 26 and 30. How did you work out the answer?

2 Find the difference, using a calculator, between 139 and 654. Does it matter which number you enter on the calculator first?

In **addition** the order of the numbers does not matter.

In **subtraction** the order of the numbers is important.

3 a 6 × 5 = _____
b 5 × 6 = _____

4 a 20 ÷ 4 = _____
b 4 ÷ 20 = a different answer!

Multiplication is the opposite of division.
3 × 5 = 15
15 ÷ 5 = 3

In **multiplication** the order of the numbers does not matter.

In **division** the order of the numbers is important.

 **Story Problems**

Select one or more arithmetic operations to solve these.

$2.00

$1.00

$2.50

50c

1 Mrs Wilson wanted every child in her class to have a new book, pencil, ruler and eraser.

a How much will each child pay?

b If there are 28 children in the class, how much money will Mrs Wilson collect from the children?

c Jeremy and Alison are twins. They brought a $20 note. How much change will Mrs Wilson give them?

2 This graph shows how quickly each child can run 50m.

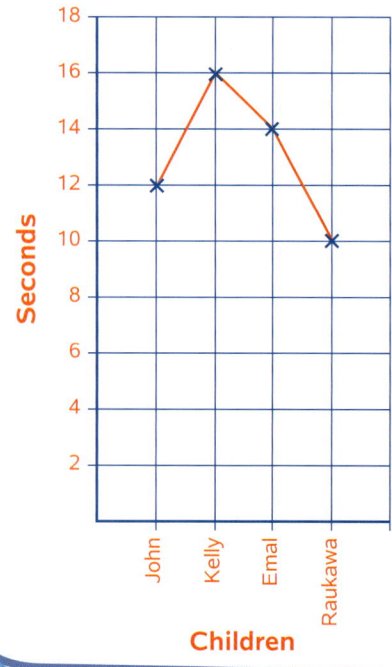

a How many seconds quicker is Raukawa than Kelly?

b If they ran a 200m relay race, running 50m each, how long would it take them?

c If the relay race took them 60 seconds to complete, and they all took the same time, how long did they each take?

d Which runner would this have been a best time for?

 **How Far?**

Auckland

127 km

Hamilton

243 km

New Plymouth

357 km

151 km

Napier

183 km

Palmerston North

Wellington

1. How far is it from Wellington to Napier?

2. A salesperson travelled from Hamilton to Palmerston North via New Plymouth and Wellington. How far did she drive?

3. The distance from Auckland to Napier is 425 km. How far is it from Hamilton to Napier?

4. The distance from Auckland to Palmerston North is 539 km. How far is it from Hamilton to Palmerston North?

5. The Spiers family were driving from New Plymouth to Wellington. They broke down a third of the way through their journey:
   a. How far had they travelled?
   b. How much further do they need to go?

Challenge

A famous pop group is planning a tour of all the towns on the map.
They are flying into and out of Wellington airport.
Plan a tour for them which goes to all the towns and covers the shortest distance.

Off to the Animal Farm

Class 4 are going on a trip to an animal farm.
They must have an adult with every 6 children.
There are 30 children in the class.

1 How many adults are needed for the trip?

2 How much is the entrance fee altogether?

Half the children have brought money for a pony ride.

3 How many children are having pony rides?

While the children are having their rides, the rest of the
children are collecting eggs. Each child collects 4 eggs.

4 How many eggs are collected?

5 The eggs are put into boxes of 6.
How many boxes are used?

The pony ride is all the way around
an oblong field.

6 How far is the pony ride?

7 Kirsty falls off her pony after 469 m
and has to walk back.
How far does she have to walk?

78 m

186 m

Challenge

**How many adults stay with the pony riders and how
many go with the egg collectors? Justify your answer.**

After lunch, a fifth of the class feed the lambs.
They are going to feed one lamb each.
Each lamb needs 150 mL of milk.

8 How much milk do they need to mix up?

The rest of the class go to see the rabbits.

9 How many children go to see the rabbits?

This is too many, so a third of them go to catch
a duckling for the heaviest duckling competition.

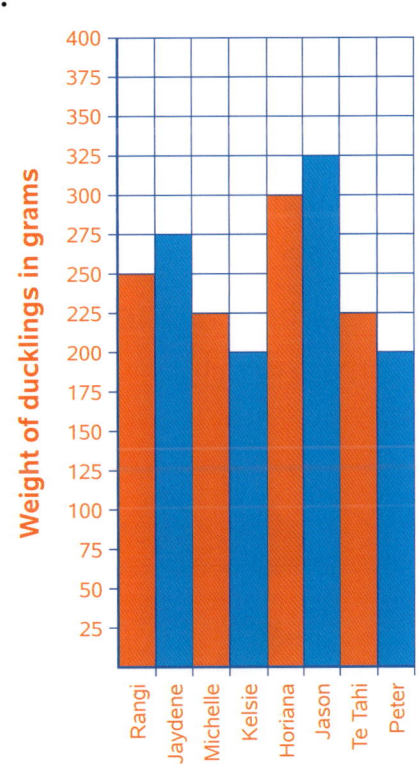

10 How many children are left with the rabbits?

11 Who catches the heaviest duckling?

12 What is the difference in weight
   between the heaviest and lightest
   duckling?

13 What is the total weight of all the
   ducklings caught?

Meanwhile, back with the rabbits –
the children have found 7 rabbits with
4 babies each.

14 How many baby rabbits are there?

15 If each child picked up a baby
   rabbit, how many baby rabbits are
   left in the cage?

 ## Open and Closed Shapes

Draw a shape or doodle on a piece of paper.

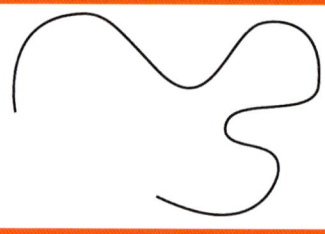

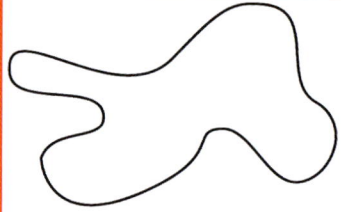

Have you drawn an open shape or a closed shape?

You will need a clean piece of paper.

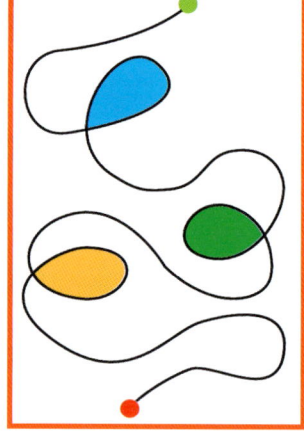

1 Put a green dot at the top of the paper.
2 Put a red dot at the bottom of the paper.
3 Take your pen or pencil for a long walk starting at the green dot and finishing at the red dot.

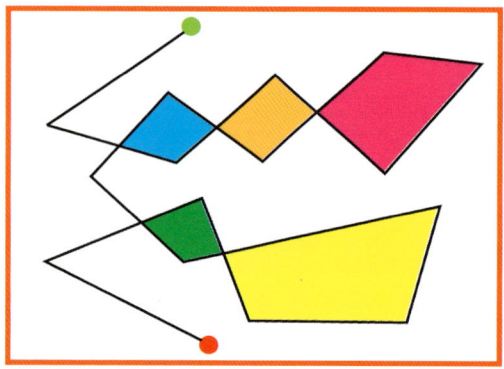

4 Use crayons to colour in all the closed shapes in your picture.

Drawing Straight Lines

To draw a straight line you will need a ruler.

Always hold your ruler in the middle and pull your pencil along the top edge.

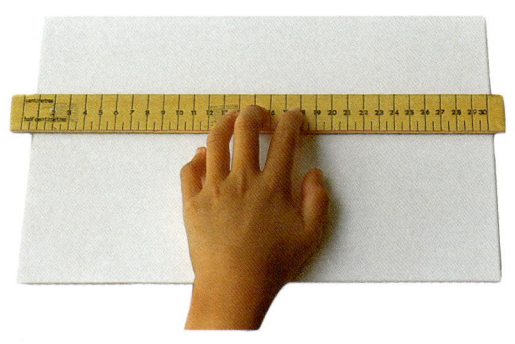

Practise drawing straight lines with your ruler and different coloured pens. When you can draw straight lines really well, try the next activity.

Design a maze

1   Use a pencil and ruler to draw a large square.
2   Mark the entrance and exit to your maze.
3   Use your ruler to mark the barriers in your maze.

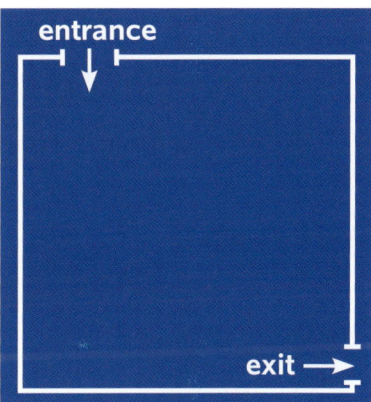

4   Which is the shortest way through your maze?
5   Can your friend find a way through your maze?

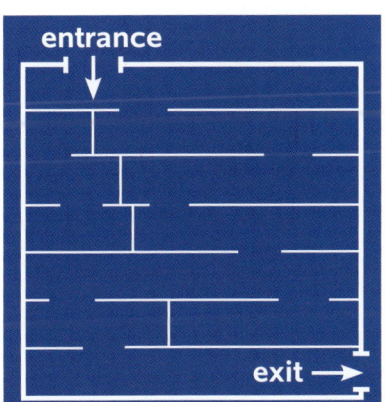

Challenge

Design a complex maze and mazes of different shapes.

Straight Lines and Closed Shapes

1 Use a ruler to draw closed shapes with straight lines.

2 What is the least number of straight lines you can use to draw a closed shape?

3 What is this shape called?

Quadrilaterals are shapes with 4 straight sides.

4 Can you name any of these shapes?

Can You Draw . . . ?

1 A pentagon has 5 straight lines.

 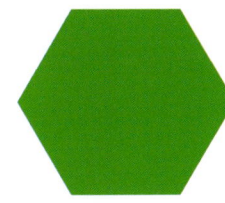 **2** A hexagon has 6 straight lines.

3 A heptagon has 7 straight lines.

 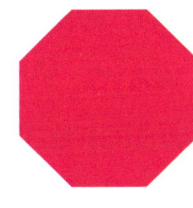 **4** An octagon has 8 straight lines.

5 A nonagon has 9 straight lines.

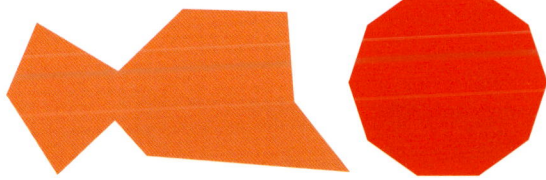

6 A decagon has 10 straight lines.

Challenge

Draw a dodecagon (a shape with 12 sides).

Looking at Straight Lines

Tie a weight to a piece of string and hold the other end of the string.
What happens to the piece of string?
It makes a straight line going up and down.

Upright lines are called vertical lines.

Half fill a glass or jar with water. Tip the glass in different ways. What do you notice about the water each time?
The water stays level. Some straight lines are neither vertical nor horizontal. They are called slanting or sloping lines.

Level lines are called horizontal lines.

Challenge

Draw a picture using only straight lines. Remember: hold your ruler in the middle and pull the pencil, don't push it.

 ## Right Angles

1 How many right angles are on the cover of this book?
2 How many right angles can you see on a door?

Use your right angle measure to test the right angles you can find in the classroom.

Challenge

Find out how a builder makes walls vertical or horizontal.

 ## Measuring a Right Angle

Find something circular like a lid of a pot.

Draw around your circle on a piece of paper.

Cut out the circle.

Fold the paper in half …

… and half again.

right angle

Label the corner.

Fit your measure carefully into each of these angles. Are they all right angles?

Squares and Oblongs

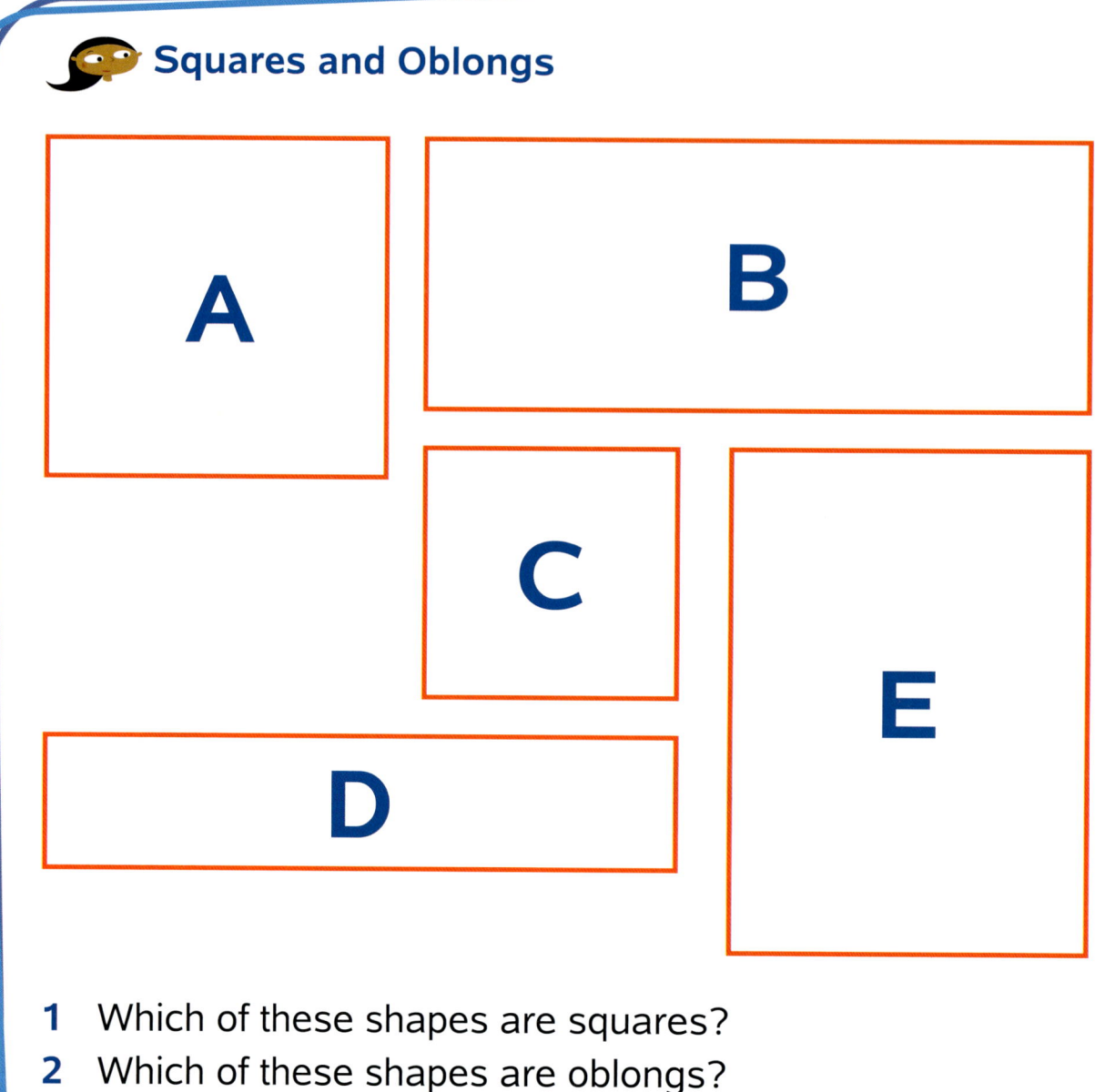

A

B

C

E

D

1 Which of these shapes are squares?

2 Which of these shapes are oblongs?

3 Use your right angle measure (from page 111) to test the corners of all the shapes.
What did you find out?

4 Copy and complete the sentence:
Squares and oblongs have four r_____ a_____ corners.

5 What is the difference between a square and an oblong?

More Squares and Oblongs

1 Find 4 strips of stiff card, all the same length, and fasten them at the corners with split pins to make a square.

2 On a piece of paper draw around the inside of your square.

3 Push the square at the corners to make a different shape.
Draw the new shape.

4 Do this again and draw the new shape.

5 Are your new shapes squares? Try to explain your answer.

6 Find 4 strips of stiff card, two long and two shorter, and fasten them at the corners with split pins to make an oblong.

7 On a piece of paper draw around the inside of your oblong.

8 Push the oblong at the corners to make a different shape. Draw the new shape.

9 Do this again and draw the new shape.

10 Are your new shapes oblongs? Try to explain your answer.

CHAPTER 19

Triangles

 Triangles All Around Us

Use 4 meccano strips or 4 strips of card joined at the corners with split pins.

1 Can you push the corners to change the shape?

Put another strip diagonally across your rectangle.

Your rectangle is now two triangles.

2 Can you push the corners to change the shape now?

Look at photographs of buildings and structures. Notice how many triangles are used.

A triangle is a very strong shape.

Challenge

How many triangles can you find in this pattern?

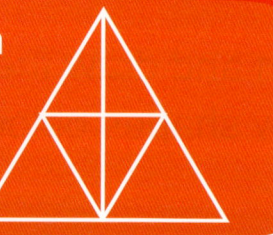

Different Sorts of Triangles

An equilateral triangle has 3 equal sides.

An isosceles triangle has 2 equal sides.

A scalene triangle has 3 different sides.

A right-angled triangle has 1 right angle.

Use a geoboard and some elastic bands to make:

1 equilateral triangles

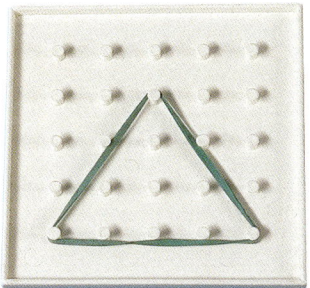

2 scalene triangles

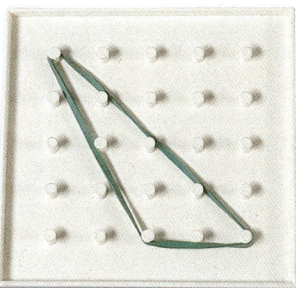

3 right angled triangles

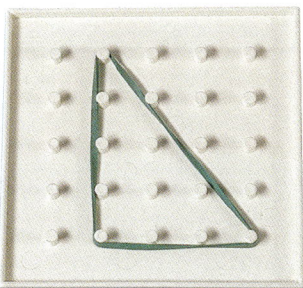

4 Can you make an isosceles triangle?

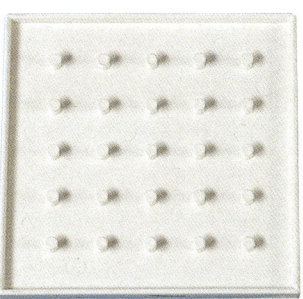

Tessellating Triangles

You will need: 4 identical isosceles triangles
6 identical equilateral triangles.

1 Fit your 4 isosceles triangles together to make a square.

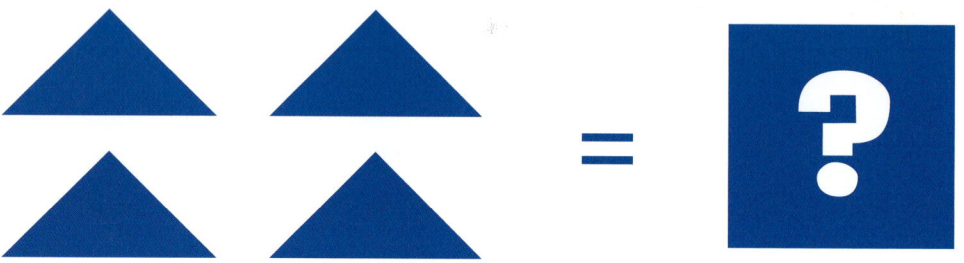

2 Use 4 equilateral triangles to make 1 large triangle.

3 Fit 6 equilateral triangles together to make a hexagon (a shape with 6 sides).

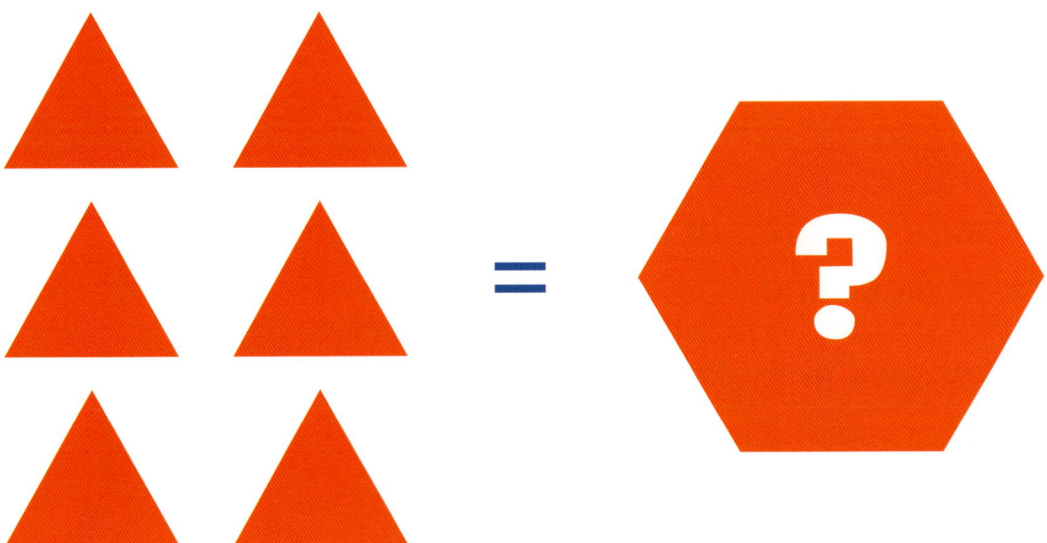

4 Investigate patterns using scalene triangles.

a

b

For each pattern, the triangles must be identical.

 **Pyramids**

A triangle is a flat shape.
A solid triangle is called a pyramid.

Make a Triangular Pyramid

You will need 6 straws of the same length and some Blu-tack or plasticine.

1 Use 3 straws to make a triangle holding the corners with Blu-tack or plasticine.

2 Stand a straw at each corner.

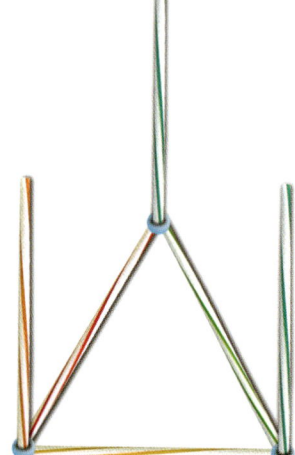

3 Pull the three standing straws together and hold with Blu-tack or plasticine.

Answer these questions.
1 How many faces has a triangular pyramid?
2 What shape are the faces?

This shape has a special name: it is a tetrahedron.

Make a Square Pyramid

You will need a 6cm square and four 6cm equilateral triangles.

1   Use Sellotape to join your shapes to make the net of a square pyramid.

2   Fold up the triangles and tape the sides.

Answer these questions.

1   How many faces has a square pyramid?

2   What are the shapes of the faces?

Challenge

Do the triangles have to be equilateral triangles? Experiment making pyramids with isosceles triangles. Remember: one side must be the same length as the side of the square.

Cross-sections are the shape of slices of a 3-dimensional shape.

The shape of a slice of bread is a cross-section of a loaf of bread.

What shape do you make if you slice:

1 A tomato?

2 A carrot?

3 An apple?

Different Cross-sections

You will need:
some potatoes and carrots, some paint or printing inks, a sharp knife (your teacher should look after this).

1 Cut your potatoes and carrots to make different shaped cross-sections.

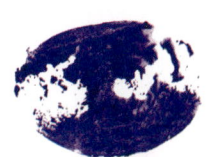

2 Use your cross-section shapes to print a pattern.
Can you make a symmetrical pattern?
Can you make a repeating pattern?

Finding Cross-sections

You will need some playdough and a blunt knife.

1 With your playdough, make 2 cylinders.

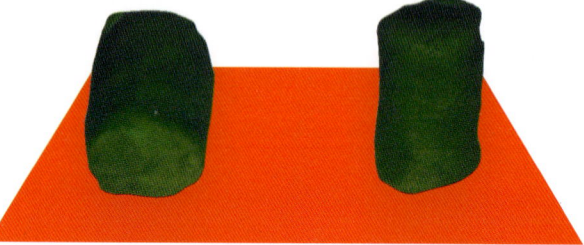

2 Cut each cylinder in half.

3 Look at the faces you have cut. What shape are they?

4 Make some more shapes with your playdough.
How many different faces can you make by cutting each shape in different ways?

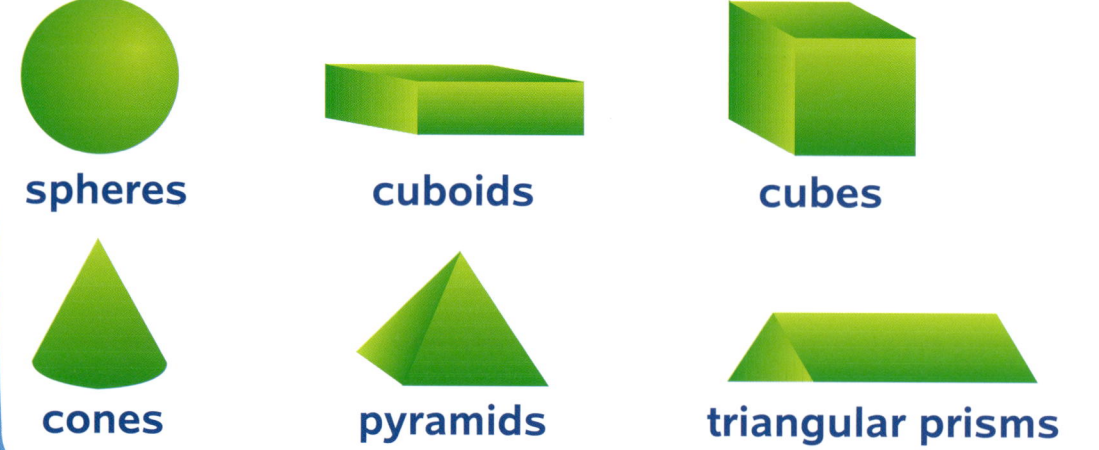

spheres   cuboids   cubes

cones   pyramids   triangular prisms

What have you found out?

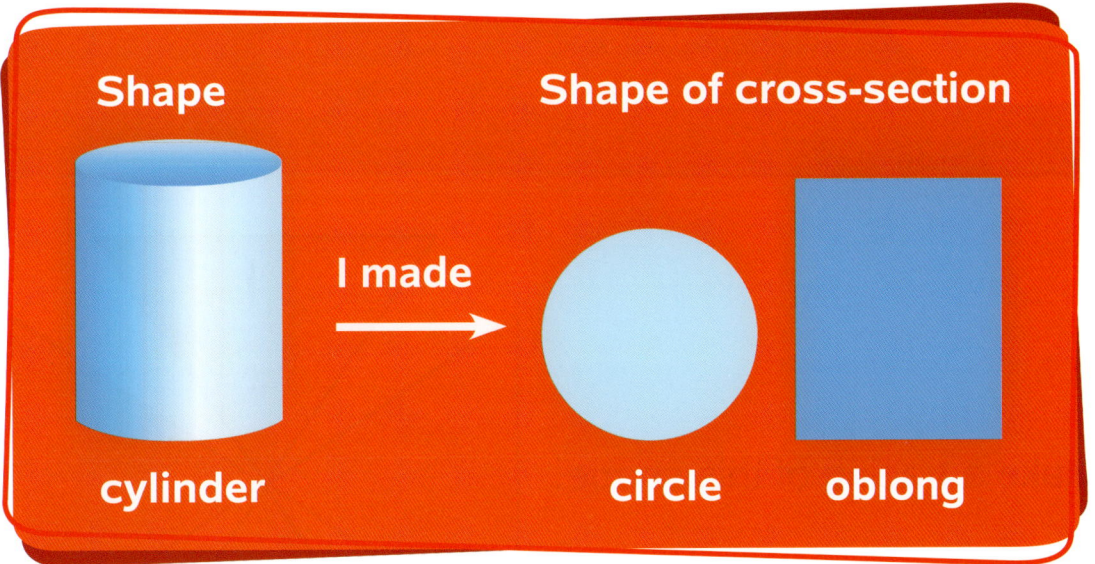

Shape	Shape of cross-section
cylinder	circle oblong

I made

Use words and pictures to show all the different cross-sections you made for each of your playdough shapes.

What shape will these cross-sections be?

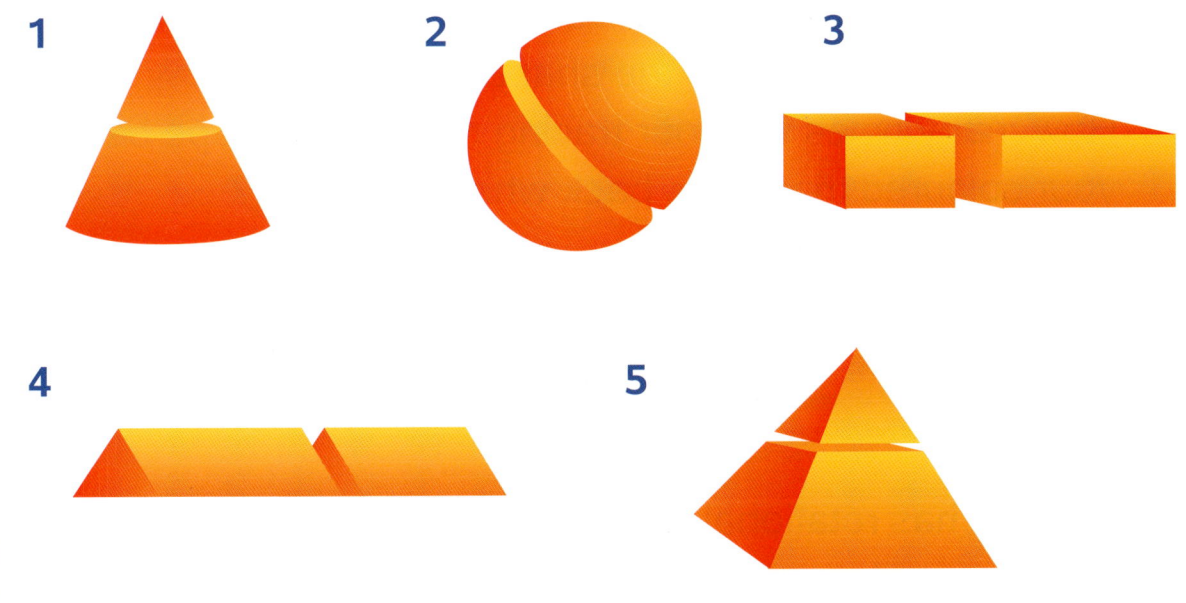

1   2   3

4   5

1   Make a tracing of this shape.

2   Colour one triangle.
3   Turn your tracing a quarter turn clockwise.
4   Will your tracing match the shape again?
5   How many times will your tracing match the shape before your coloured triangle is back where it started?

A shape that can be rotated (turned) about a centre point, and matches the shape a number of times in a complete turn, is said to have rotational symmetry.

This shape has rotational symmetry of order 4.
(It matches its shape 4 times.)

6 Find the order of rotational symmetry in each of these shapes. Trace each shape and rotate.

Make Amazing Shapes with Rotational Symmetry

1. Draw a shape on a piece of card. It may have curved lines or straight lines or both. Make it simple enough to cut out.
2. Cut out the shape and put a drawing pin through the middle of your shape.

3. Pin your shape on a piece of paper. (Put a pile of newspaper or a pinboard under your paper.)
4. Draw around your shape.

5. Rotate your shape a quarter turn around the pin and draw around it again.
6. Rotate another quarter turn and draw around your shape again.

7 Rotate another quarter turn and draw around your shape again.

8 Lift your shape off the paper. Use a coloured pen to draw around the edge of the shape you have created.

9 Cut out the shape, turn it over so you can't see the pencil lines and stick it onto another piece of paper.

Your shape has rotational symmetry of order 4.

Challenge

Can you create a shape with rotational symmetry of order 8?

Kowhaiwhai Patterns

Kowhaiwhai are the patterns used to decorate the rafters of the wharenui on marae.

Design a koru pattern.

starting pattern

Translating

Begin with the starting koru pattern, move it along and copy it.

 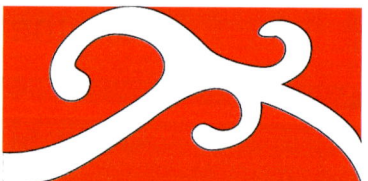 

Reflecting

Begin with the starting koru pattern, reflect (flip) it and copy.

flip and copy   **flip and copy**

Rotating

Start with a koru pattern that begins in the middle of the left side and finishes in the middle of the right side.

 Draw the pattern again making it a half turn different.

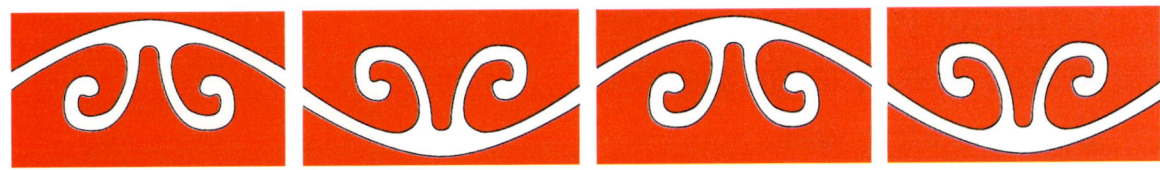

Make up your own kowhaiwhai patterns using translating, reflecting and rotating.

You might use the same koru pattern for each.

Which design do you like best?

CHAPTER 22

Enlargements

Enlargements

1 Draw a simple, closed shape using straight lines and curved lines.
2 Cut out your shape.
3 Put your shape on an overhead projector (OHP) and project the image onto a large piece of paper on the wall.
4 Draw around the image on the wall.
5 Cut out this shape.
6 Compare your two shapes. One should be an exact enlargement of the other.

Experiment with different shapes.
Try moving the OHP closer to the wall and then further away from the wall.

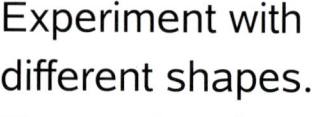

Challenge

Make a set of at least 5 shapes, which are all different sizes of the same shape.

Balloon Enlargements

You will need two deflated balloons.

1 With a thick felt pen, write your name on one of the balloons.

2 Now blow up your balloon.

What has happened to your name?

3 Blow up the other balloon and ask a friend to hold the neck while you write your name with a thick felt pen.

4 Now carefully let the air out of your balloon. What has happened to your name?

 **Flight Paths**

1 Blow up a balloon.
2 Let the balloon go. Which way did it go?
3 Try it again. Did it go the same way?

The way the balloon travels is its flight path.
You don't know what the flight path will be
until the balloon has travelled it. For many objects,
the flight path will always be the same.

water out of a hosepipe

bouncing a ball

Knowing about flight paths is very important when playing games like netball or rugby.
Try throwing a ball to make these flight paths.

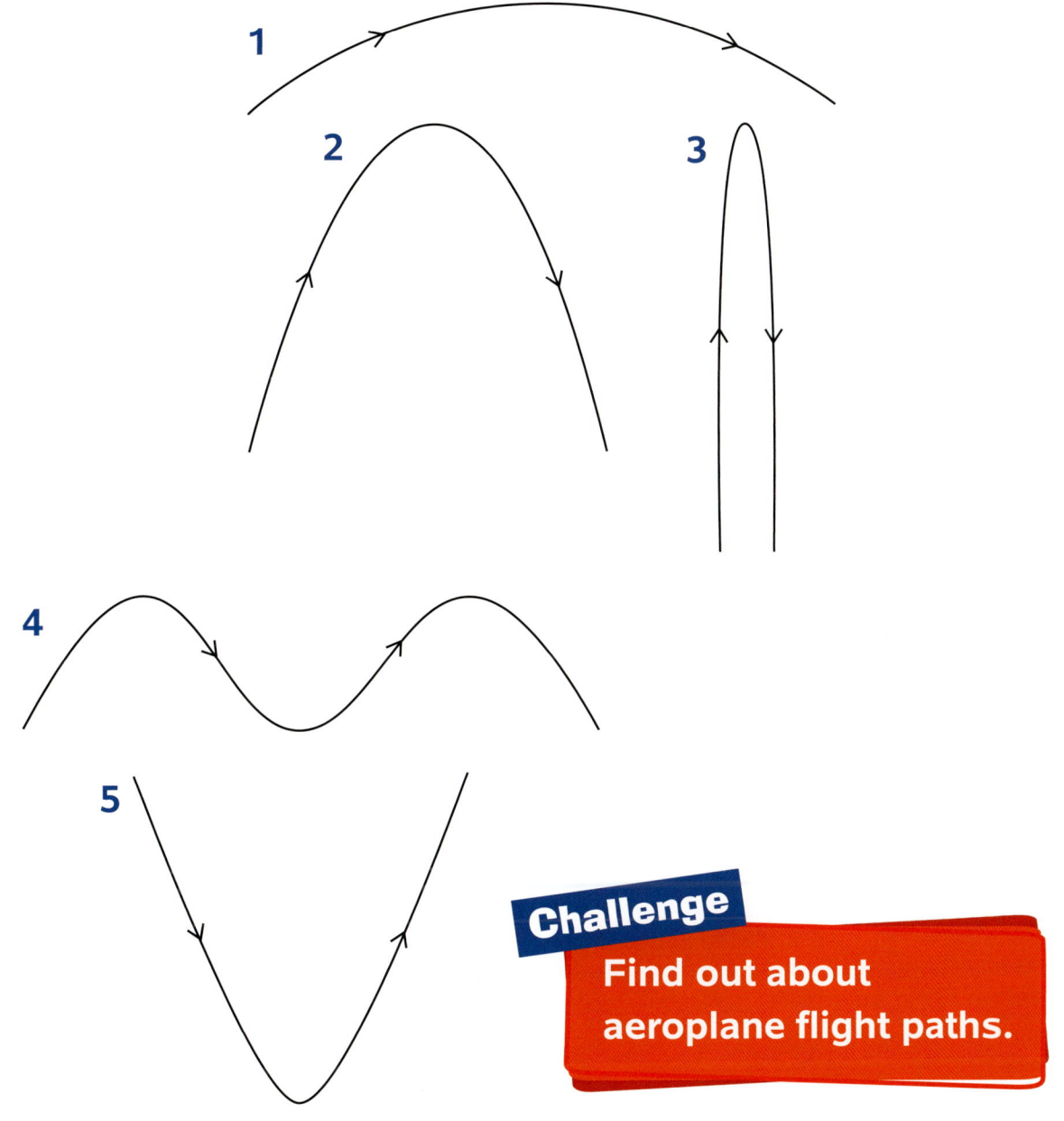

Challenge

Find out about aeroplane flight paths.

CHAPTER 23

Giving Directions: N S E W

Look at a globe. The North Pole is at the top. The South Pole is at the bottom. Maps are usually drawn with North at the top and South at the bottom.

Look on a world map or globe.

1   If you travel North from New Zealand, which country would you reach?

2   If you travel East from New Zealand, which country would you reach?

3   What country lies to the West of New Zealand?

N

W ← → E

West is to the left

East is to the right

S

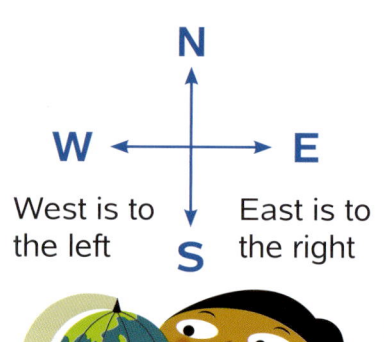

THE WORLD

Challenge

How can you find out which way is North on a sunny day?

Using a Compass

Which way is North in your classroom?
Use a compass to find out.

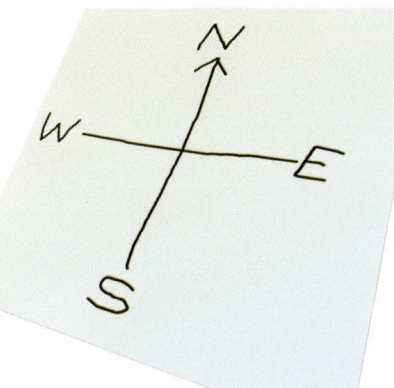

1 Draw a compass on a piece of paper.
2 Put your piece of paper on the floor
   with North pointing to the North.

Which way are you facing?

1 Face North.
   Make a quarter
   turn to your left.

2 Face East.
   Make a quarter
   turn clockwise.

3 Face South.
   Make a half turn
   to your right.

4 Face West.
   Make a three-quarter
   turn anticlockwise.

5 Face North.
   Make a half turn to your left.

 **Which Direction?**

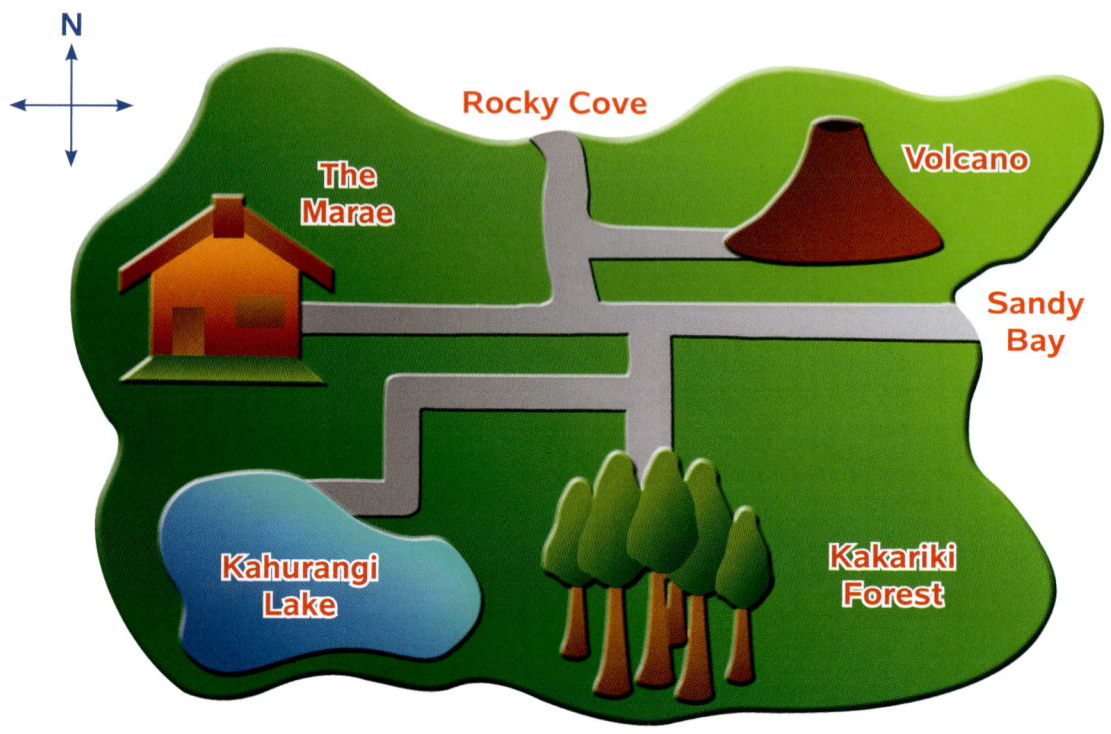

The Raiwhara family are staying on the marae.
They want to visit some of the places on the island.
Awanui gave them directions to Rocky Cove.

Drive east out of the marae.
Turn left and drive north to Rocky Cove.

Write the Raiwhara family directions from:

1   Rocky Cove to the volcano.
2   The volcano to Sandy Bay.
3   Sandy Bay back to the marae.

4 The next day the Raiwhara family want to do some sailing on Kahurangi Lake. Can you give the directions to get to the lake?

5 Mr Raiwhara took his family on a mystery tour after leaving the lake. He drove east, turned left and drove north. He made a quarter turn clockwise and drove east, then he turned right.

Which direction is he travelling?
Where has he taken his family?

Give the Raiwhara family directions
to get back to the marae.

The Eight Points of the Compass

To give even better directions, the compass names the directions halfway between the four points of the compass.

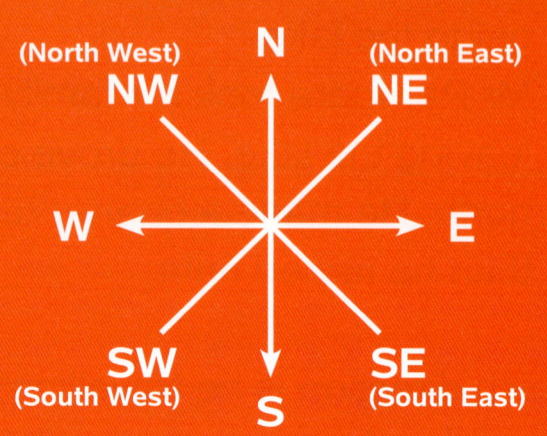

1   On your floor compass, add the directions north east, north west, south east, south west.

2   Name an object in your classroom at each of the eight directions on your compass.

3   Play 'I spy' giving the direction you are 'spying' as a clue instead of the first letter.

Challenge

Draw an eight-pointed compass on the school playground.
Make up a game using the compass.

Which town is:

1 South of Auckland?

2 North of Rotorua?

3 West of Wellington?

4 East of Hamilton?

5 North east of Napier?

6 South west of Christchurch?

7 South east of New Plymouth?

8 North west of Christchurch?

9 South west of Napier?

10 North east of Invercargill?

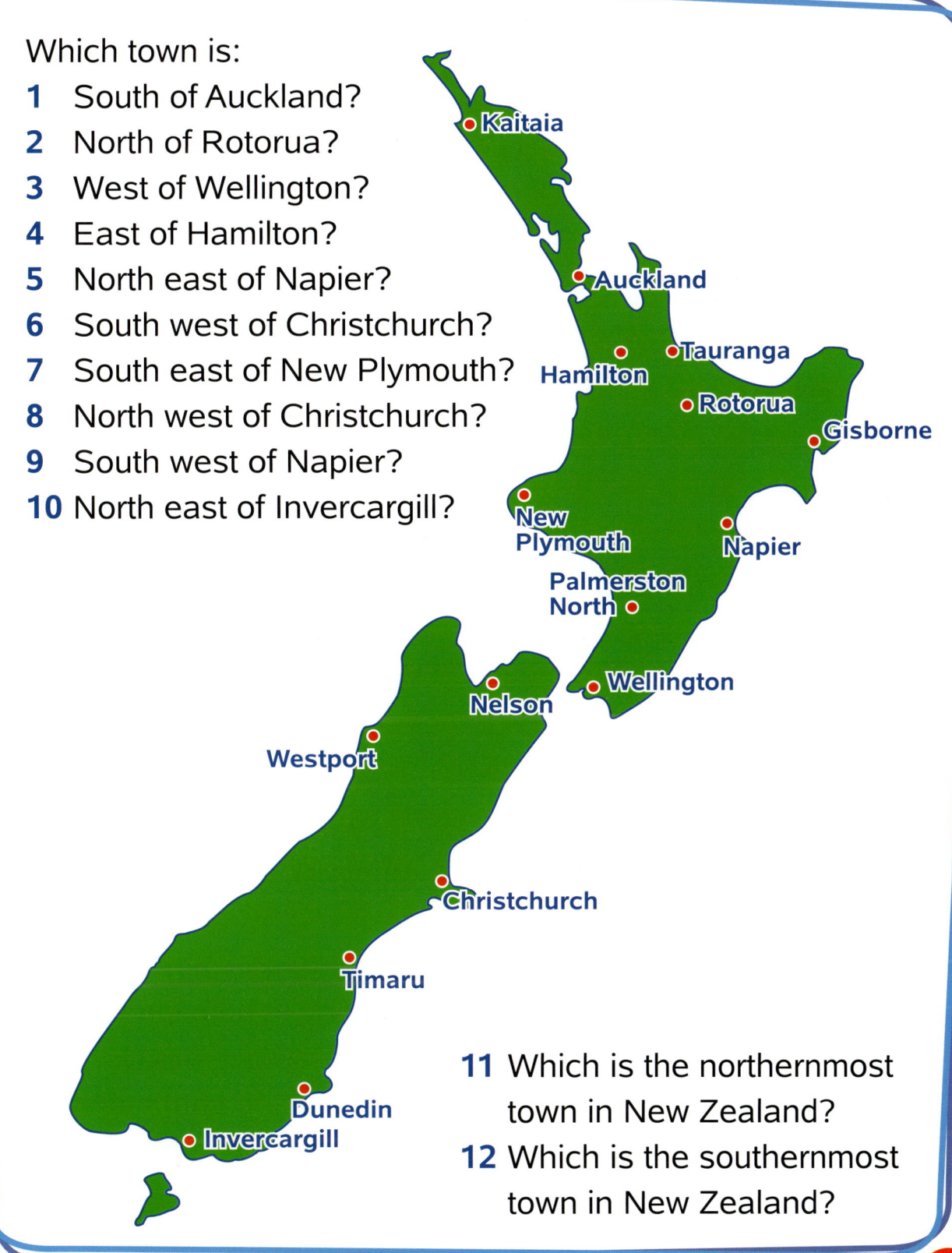

11 Which is the northernmost town in New Zealand?

12 Which is the southernmost town in New Zealand?

Treasure Hunt

N

W ← → E

S

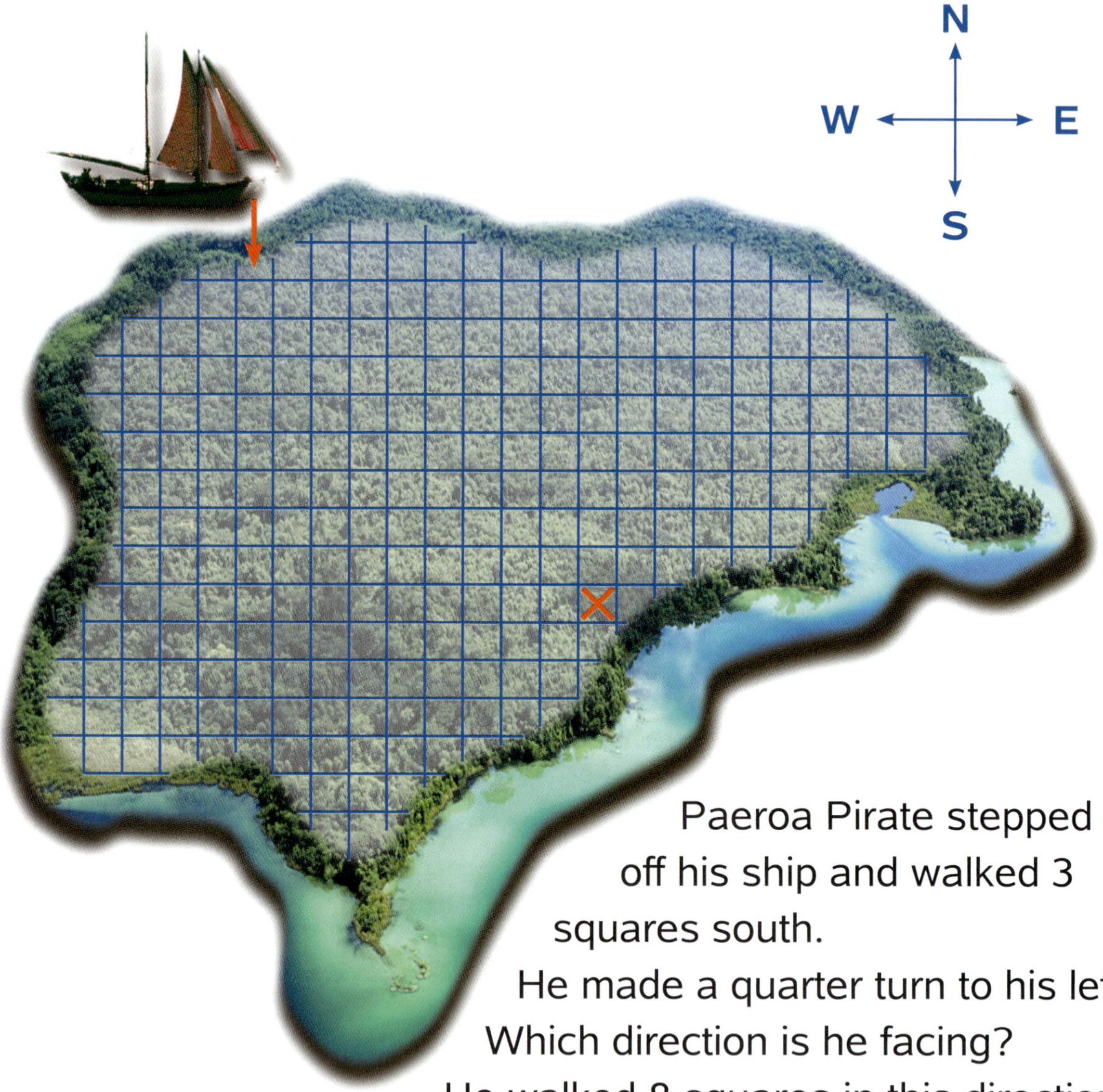

Paeroa Pirate stepped off his ship and walked 3 squares south.

He made a quarter turn to his left. Which direction is he facing?

He walked 8 squares in this direction.

Which way did he turn to be facing south again?

Give Paeroa Pirate more directions to help him reach his buried treasure.

Choose another square on the island to bury some treasure in.

Give Paeroa Pirate directions from his ship to the new buried treasure.

Draw an island of your own on squared paper. Bury some treasure somewhere on your island. You might like to add some other landmarks on your map, for example a cabin, a lake, a landing strip for an aircraft, a safe harbour for a ship.

Choose a starting point (depends if you arrived by ship or plane!) and write a list of directions to find your treasure.

Give your map and list of directions to a friend and see if they can follow your directions to find the treasure.

CHAPTER 24

Using a Ruler to Measure Length

You will need some centimetre cubes.

Use the cm cubes to measure these lines.

Remember to start the cubes at one end of the line.

1 Line A measures _____ cubes

2 Line B measures _____ cubes

3 Line C measures _____ cubes

A ruler is a measuring instrument that has all the measuring units (centimetres) joined together.

The measure starts with the 0.

Be careful – this is often not right at the end of the ruler.

Match the 0 up to the beginning of the line you want to measure and read the number off the ruler at the other end of the line.

Measure the lines again using your ruler.

4 Line A measures _____ cm

5 Line B measures _____ cm

6 Line C measures _____ cm.

Why did you get the same answers as when you measured with the cubes?

Measuring with a Ruler

Practice using a ruler to measure length.

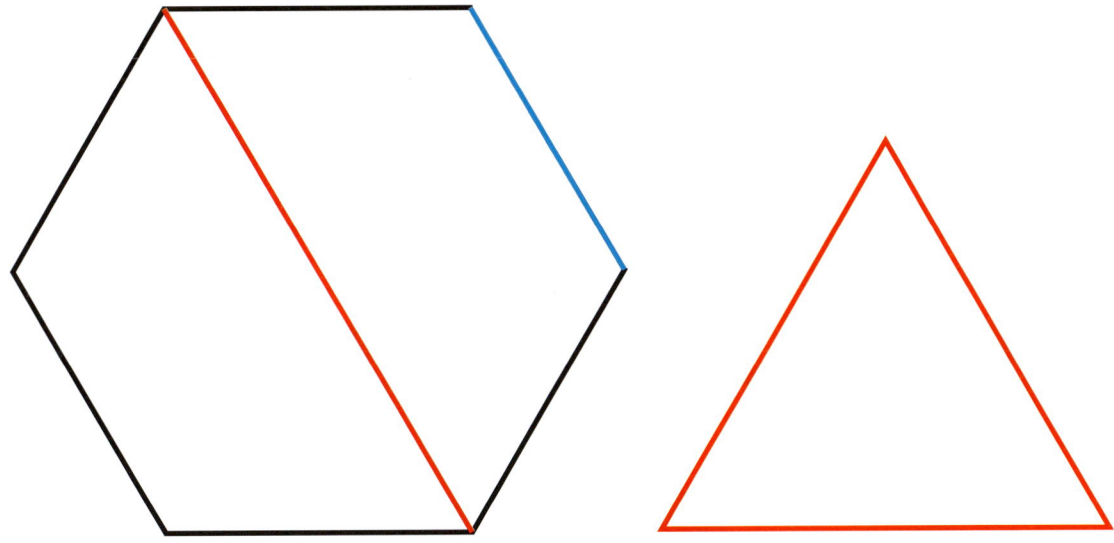

Measure the sides of the hexagon.

1   Each side measures _____ cm
2   How long is the red line inside the hexagon, to the nearest whole centimetre?

The red line is _____ cm long.

3   Are all the sides of the triangle the same length?

Side 1 measures _____ cm
Side 2 measures _____ cm
Side 3 measures _____ cm

Different Sorts of Triangles

Use your ruler to measure the sides of each triangle.

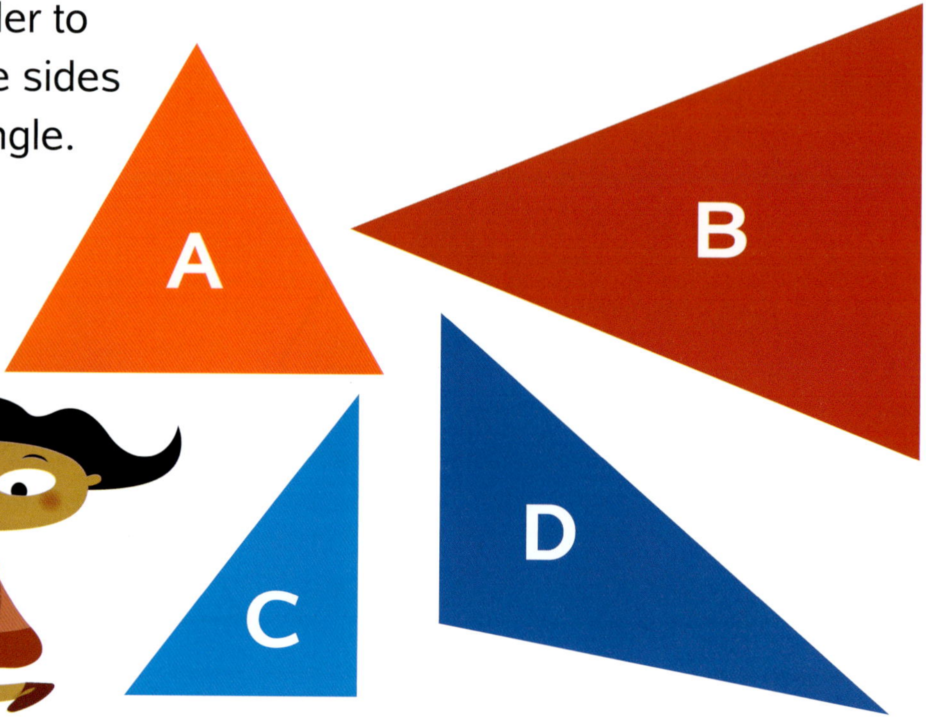

A

B

C

D

Record your results in a table.

Triangle	Side 1	Side 2	Side 3	Type of triangle
A	_____ cm	_____ cm	_____ cm	equilateral
B	_____ cm	_____ cm	_____ cm	isosceles
C	_____ cm	_____ cm	_____ cm	right-angled
D	_____ cm	_____ cm	_____ cm	scalene

Estimating and Measuring

1 Look at your ruler and find out how long 10 cm is.
Find 5 objects you estimate to be about 10 cm long.

Use your ruler to measure and complete. Copy the table
into your book.

Object	Estimate	Actual Measure
	10cm	_____ cm
	10cm	_____ cm
	10cm	_____ cm
	10cm	_____ cm
	10cm	_____ cm

2 Copy the following table into your book.

Object	Estimate	Actual Measure

Find five different objects and estimate their length in
centimetres. Then measure their length with your ruler.
Complete the table for all five objects.

Adding and Subtracting Measurements

Find three coloured pencils.

1 What is the total length of all three pencils?

_____ cm + _____ cm + _____ cm = _____ cm

2 What is the difference in length between the longest pencil and the shortest pencil?

3 Measure your handspan. What is the total length of both your handspans?

4 Measure the distance from your wrist to the top of your middle finger.
  a What is the difference between this measurement and your handspan?
  b Which is longer?

5 Measure each of your fingers on one hand. If you could put your fingers end to end, how long would it measure?

6 What is the difference in length between your longest and shortest fingers?

Finding Perimeters

The perimeter is the distance all the way around the edge of a closed shape.

Measure the length of each side and add the measurements together to find the perimeter.

1 Find the perimeter of each of these shapes:

How could multiplication help you instead of measuring each side?

2 Write a rule for finding the perimeter of a square that uses multiplication.

3 Write a rule for finding the perimeter of a rectangle that uses multiplication and addition.

4 Is multiplication useful for finding the perimeter of a triangle? Explain your answer.

Challenge

Find the perimeter of your classroom. What units will you use?

CHAPTER 25

Measuring Mass

 Kilograms and Grams

The standard units of measure for mass are the kilogram and the gram.

The prefix 'kilo' means 1000, so kilogram means 1000g.

How many grams in:

1 2kg   **2** 4kg   **3** 5kg   **4** 20kg   **5** 15kg

How many kilograms and grams in each of these weights?

6 3400g   **7** 2150g   **8** 4675g   **9** 2500g   **10** 16 400g

Ask your teacher for a kilogram weight and a $\frac{1}{2}$kg (500g) weight.

Think of some objects you think would weigh about the same as each of these weights.

Challenge

What do you think kilometre means?
What do you think kilojoule means?
Find out what this is a measure of.

Kilograms and Grams

Your teacher will give you a selection of labeled bags or objects.

Copy the following table. Estimate the weight of each object and write the name of the object or the label in the correct place on the table.

Under 500g	Between 500g and 1kg (1000g)	Between 1500g (1½kg) and 2kg (2000g)	Between 2kg (2000g) and 2500g (2½ kg)	Between 2½ kg (2500g) and 3kg (3000g)

Does everyone in your group agree?
What sort of measuring device could you use to check your results?

How Heavy is a Kilogram?

You will need a plastic carrier bag each.

1   Fill your bag with objects until you estimate it weighs
    1 kilogram.

Check with a friend by comparing your bags.
Do your bags weigh about the same?

Check the weight of your bag on a
measuring device.

2   Add or take away objects until your bag measures as
    close as you can get to one kilogram.

3   Make a list of all the objects you had in your bag.
    Sort the objects in order of weight. Estimate how many
    grams each object would weigh.

The total estimated weight of all your objects should be
1000g

Record your estimates as an addition.

_____ + _____ + _____ = 1000g

Ways to Measure Mass

You will need a selection of weighing devices.

Look at each of the measuring devices and discuss how you would use them to measure mass.

If you have digital scales, explain what the numbers mean.

If you have device with a scale, explain how to read the scale.

If you have a balance and weights, explain how to use it for measuring mass and not just comparing mass.

Using the different measuring devices, practise measuring the mass of a variety of objects.

CHAPTER 26

Area

 ## Measuring Area

Area is the measure of the surface of an object.
Look at a book. It has four edges. You could measure the edges with a ruler. (You would be measuring the perimeter.)
Put your hand on the surface of the book.

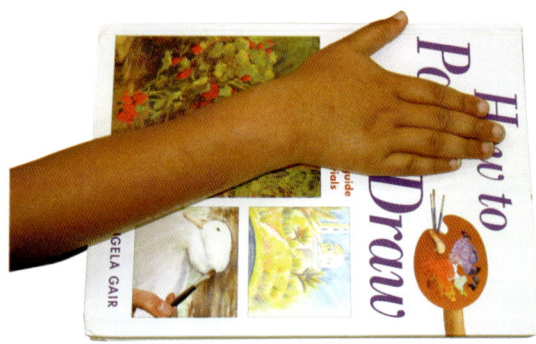

The book has a bigger area than your hand.
Find some objects with an area about
the same size as your hand.
Find some objects with an
area about the same size
as two of your hands.

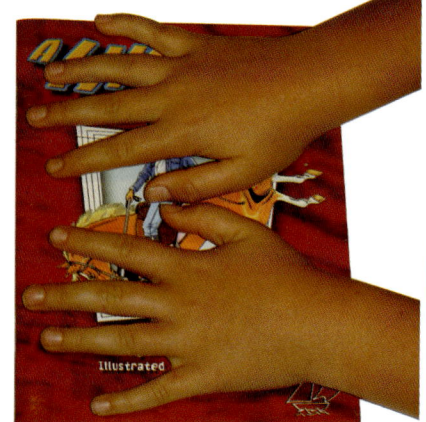

To measure area you need a unit that has a surface.
Use counters to cover each of the shapes below.
How many counters did you use?

The area of the square is _____ counters.
The area of the rectangle is _____ counters.
The area of the hexagon is _____ counters.

Do you think circles are a good measuring unit for area?
Why not?

 **Units of Measure**

Any shape that fits together without leaving spaces can be used for measuring area.
You will need some hundred squares
as your measuring units.

1 How many 100 squares will cover your desk?
My desk has an area of about _____ squares.

2 How many squares cover the seat of your chair?
My chair has an area of about _____ squares.

Find some other objects to find the area of.
Estimate the area first.
How many squares do you think you will use?

Copy and complete the table.

Object	Estimate	Measurement

Challenge

What other shapes could you use to measure area with? Look in the mosaic shape box.

Counting Squares

Kahu drew around his hand on a piece of squared paper.

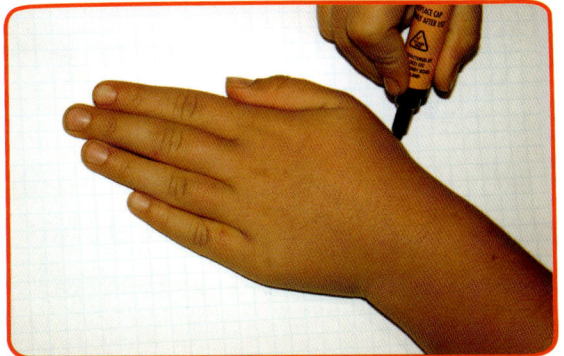

He counted all the complete squares (and the nearly complete squares) to find the area of his hand.
You will need some squared paper.
Draw around your hand and count the squares to find the area of your hand.
Do you or your friend have the bigger hand?

Draw around your foot and count the number of squares to find the area of your foot.

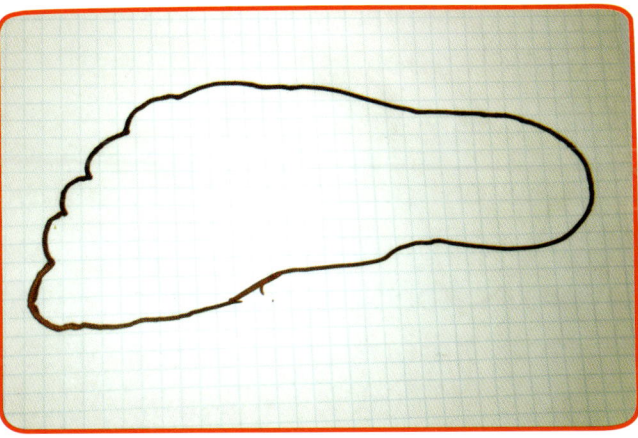

Comparing Areas

Keegan and Tui were trying to find a library book to fit in their school bags. Some books were too long and some were too wide. Their teacher suggested they should measure the area of each book.

'area' means 'the surface of'

Keegan measured the books with squares from the mosaic shapes. This graph shows what he found out.

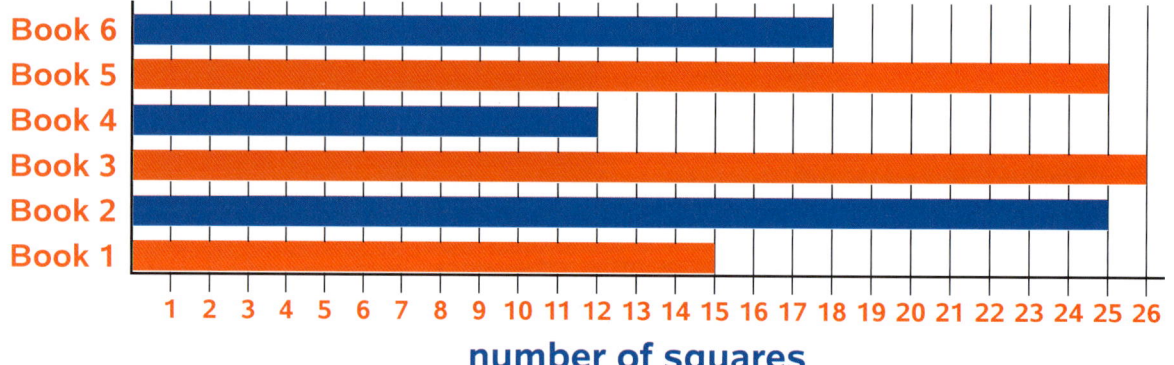

number of squares

1 Which book has the largest area?

2 Which book is the smallest?

True or false?

3 area of book 3 > area of book 1

4 area of book 3 < area of book 5

5 area of book 5 = area of book 6

6 area of book 2 > area of book 4

7 area of book 4 < area of book 6

8 area of book 2 = area of book 5

9 What is the area of book 1?

Tui measured the same
books with triangles from the mosaic shapes.
This graph shows what she found out.

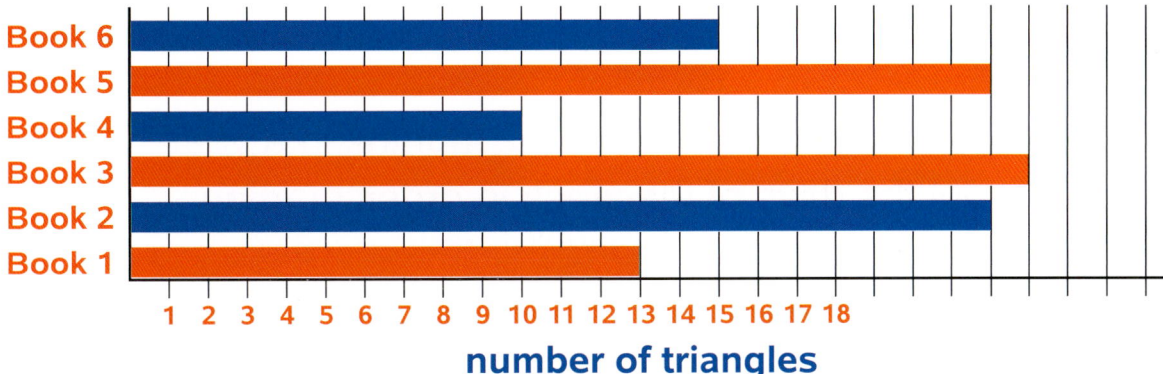

number of triangles

10 Which book is the biggest book?

11 Which book has the smallest area?

12 What is the area of book 1?

Why did Keegan and Tui get a different answer for the area
of the books? Discuss with your teacher.
Work with a friend.
Choose six different-sized books from the classroom.
Choose a different shape each to measure the areas.
Make sure you use a shape that tessellates.

Show your results on a bar graph.
Compare your graphs.
Write some statements about your
graphs using the signs <, >, =.
Can you tell from your graphs who used
the biggest shape for measuring?

CHAPTER 27

Units of Time

 Days, Months and Years

There are 7 days in a week and 12 months in a year.

1 Write out the days of the week in order, starting with Monday.

2 Write out the months of the year in order, starting with January.

Challenge

What are the Maori words for the days of the week and the months of the year?

3 How many days in each month?

Use a calendar to find out how many days in each month. Discuss why there is not the same number of days in every month.

4 Using your information and a calculator, work out how many days in one year.

Challenge

Find out about leap years.

Measuring Time in Months or Years

Sometimes we measure time in months and sometimes in years. You need to be able to change between the units.

1 Michel is 18 months old.
How many candles will he have
on his cake next birthday?

2 How many years interest free
is being offered in the sale?

3 How many months' figures is
the boss asking for when he
asks for a quarterly report?

**24 months
interest free**

4 How many months figures
would the boss be asking
for in a half-yearly report?

5 How old are you in years and months?

6 How many months old are you?

Measuring Time in Days and Hours

A day is broken up into units called hours.

1 How many hours in 1 day?

One full day is a period of daytime and a period of night-time.

Time is controlled by the way in which the Earth is turning, so it is not the same time in all parts of the world at the same time!

Monday	Tuesday	Wednesday	Thursday	Friday	Saturday	Sunday

2 Investigate the world clock on the internet and find out the time in different parts of the world. It might even be a different day!

3 a You can hire a new release DVD for 3 days.
How many hours can you have the DVD for?
b If the film was 3 hours long, how many times could you watch the film if you did nothing else?
c Explain why it is unlikely you could watch the film this number of times.

Measuring Times in Hours and Minutes

- There are exactly 12 months in 1 year.
- There are 28, 29, 30 or 31 days in a month.
- There is not a whole number of weeks in a month (except February).
- There are 7 days in a week.
- There are 24 hours in a day.
- There are 60 minutes in an hour.

What a lot to remember!

A digital clock shows time in hours and minutes.

How many hours and how many minutes are shown on each of these digital clocks?

1    2

3    4

Digital clocks are everywhere these days – make a list of all the places where you can find a digital clock.

Challenge

What is the next smaller unit of time? How many of them make 1 minute?

CHAPTER 28

Telling the Time

 **What's the Time?**

Why is it useful to be able to tell the time?

Make a list of all the important times in your day.

- Time to get up.
- Time to go to school.

We learn to tell the time so we know when it is time to do something or to be able to work out how much time we have before we need to do something.

To measure time we use either:

an analogue clock    or   a digital clock

Which clocks are saying the same time?

a

b

c

d

e

f

Half and Quarter Past

In Book 2a you learnt to read half past the hour and quarter past the hour on a clock face.

At what number is the minute hand (the longer hand) pointing to at
a o'clock?
b half past the hour?
c quarter past the hour?

Is the number the minute hand is pointing to important, or its position on the clock?
Explain your answer.

Ask your teacher for a photocopy of the page of clock faces.
Draw the hands to show the following times:
1 4 o'clock
2 half past 8
3 quarter past 5

Did you remember to make sure your hour hand (the smaller hand) was only pointing exactly to the hour at the o'clock time?
At half past the hour the hour hand is also halfway between the hours, and at quarter past the hour hand is a quarter of the way past the hour.

60 minutes in 1 hour.
30 minutes in half and hour.
15 minutes in quarter of an hour.

Find the matching clocks:

a

b

c

d

e

f

g

h

i

j

k

l

Reading Minutes Past the Hour

1 How many minutes in one hour?

It takes the minute hand one hour to move all the way around the clock.

2 How many small segments are marked around the edge of the clock face?

Each of these segments measures 1 minute.

3 How many minutes would have passed if the hand moves from pointing at 12 to pointing at 1?

This clock reads 5 minutes past 7.
We most often say 5 past 7.

4 How many minutes would have passed if the hand moves from pointing at 12 to pointing at 2?

This clock reads 10 minutes past 7 or 10 past 7.

The minute hand is counting the small segments, the minutes. The big numbers on the clock are for the hours only.

5 Which multiplication table can help you read the minutes on a clock face?

Minutes Past on a Digital Clock

A digital clock always uses two digits
for the minutes.
Five minutes past
seven looks like:

Write these times as digital times, and as how you would
say the time.

1

2

3

4

5

6

7

8

9

10

Reading Digital Time

The digital clock shows all time by counting the minutes past the hour.

This clock says 35 minutes past 4:

1 What are the most minutes past an hour you could read on a digital clock?

You will need a clock face with moveable hands and a partner to work with. With your partner, work out what an analogue clock would look like for the following digital times.

2 5:35 **3** 8:50 **4** 7:40 **5** 3:45 **6** 2:55

Think very carefully where the hour hand will be pointing as well as the minute hand.

Draw the hands for each of the times on clock faces.
(Ask your teacher for a photocopy sheet.)

Did you think to use your five times table to help you?

8 x 5 = 40

Minutes To on the Analogue Clock

You already know how an analogue clock looks for the time 4:35, and to read the time as 35 minutes past 4 is correct – BUT we normally read the time as the number of minutes TO the next hour.

You already know there are 5 minutes between each of the numbers on the clock.
Count in fives from the number 7 to the number 12.

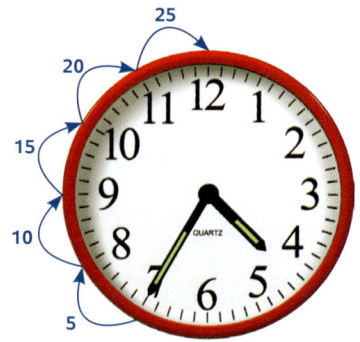

35 minutes past 4 is the same as 25 minutes to 5.

Use a clock face to make these times, and then write the time as minutes to the next hour.

1 35 minutes past 6 = 25 minutes to _____

2 40 minutes past 3 = _____

3 55 minutes past 9 = _____

4 45 minutes past 7 = _____

5 50 minutes past 2 = _____

Telling the Time

For each of the times, write the digital time in numbers and words and how you would say the time.

Example:  ⟶ 5:10 ⟶ five ten ⟶ ten past five

1

2

3

4

5

6

7

8

9

10

11

12

CHAPTER 29

Sorting Information

 ## Designing Tables

A table is a way of sorting information or data to be collected. It is made up of columns and rows.

Use a Word document on a computer.
Go to Table and click Insert Table.

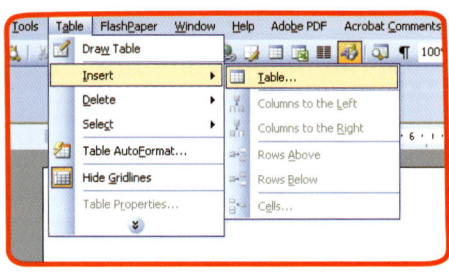

Think about the information you need to collect to decide how many columns and rows your table will need. (On a computer you can add or delete columns and rows if you change your mind!)

Each column in a table must have a heading.

Design a table to collect the following data.
(Either on paper, using a ruler or on computer.)

Everybody's name, age, favourite colour and if they are left handed or right handed.

Compare your table with someone else. Are they exactly the same or could they be slightly different?

Look at the following table

Name	Girl or Boy	Age	Birth Month	Eye Colour
Emily	Girl	16	December	Blue
Kristina	Girl	12	November	Brown
Jonathon	Boy	14	November	Blue
William	Boy	11	April	Blue
Rachel	Girl	15	October	Blue
Emma	Girl	13	May	Brown
Arwen	Girl	11	March	Brown
Bethan	Girl	6	March	Brown
Megan	Girl	11	February	Blue
Julie	Girl	9	February	Blue
Sarah	Girl	8	November	Blue
Nathan	Boy	8	November	Blue
Joshua	Boy	10	January	Brown
Ben	Boy	7	December	Brown

Read each sentence and use the table to say whether the statement is true or false.

1 William has blue eyes.
2 If you are born in March you have brown eyes.
3 There are more boys born in November than girls.
4 The oldest person is a girl with blue eyes.
5 The youngest person is a boy with brown eyes.
6 William was born in April.
7 The youngest boy was born in December.
8 All eight-year-olds were born in November.

Other ways of sorting help you to see information even more clearly.

Designing Tables on a Spreadsheet

Open a spreadsheet on a computer. You will see the spreadsheet is made up of columns and rows like a table. Each space in the table is called a cell.

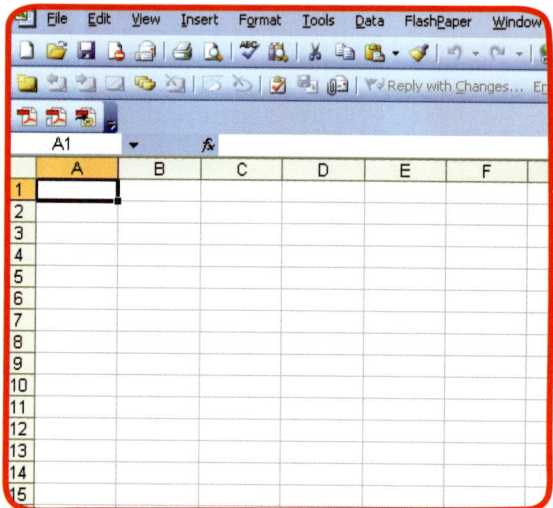

You can type words or numbers in each cell.

Type your name in one cell and your age in another cell. What do you notice?

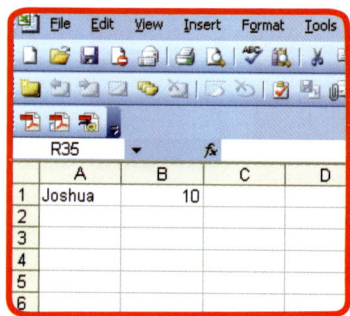

Type the information of the first 7 rows of the table on page 171 onto a spreadsheet.

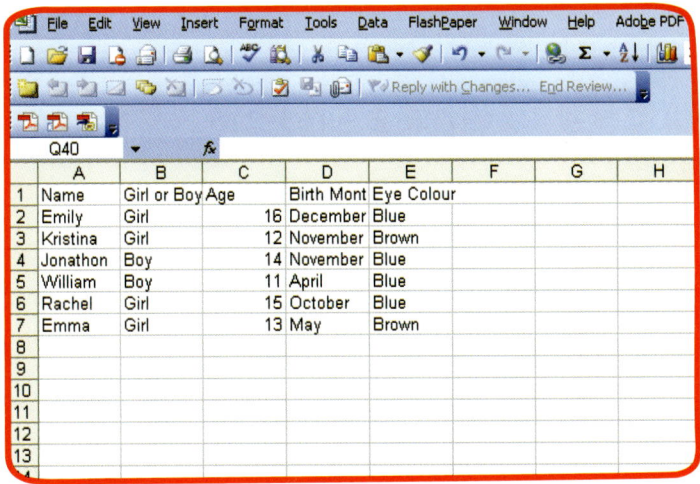

Place the cursor between the letters on the top row, then click and drag to widen the columns if necessary.

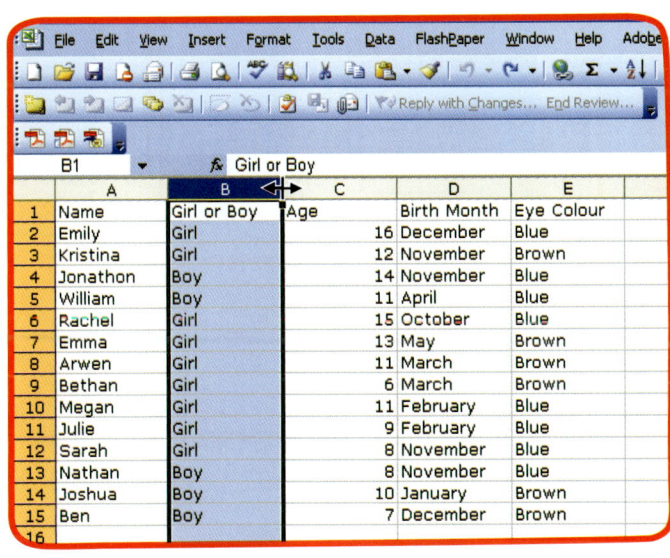

When all your data is in the table, use the cursor to left click and drag across the table from top left to bottom right to highlight the whole table.

Click on the following sequence to draw a grid for your table.

Click Format

Click Cells

Click Borders

Click Outline and Inside

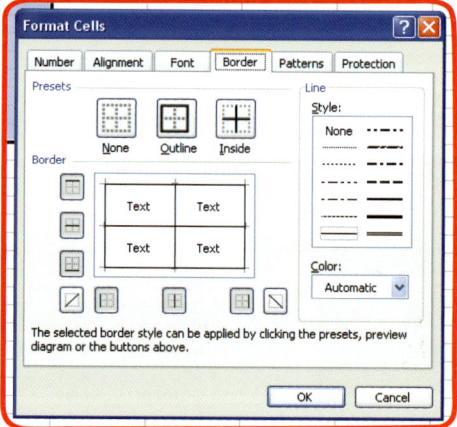

Click OK.

Your table should now have the grid lines between the rows and columns drawn in.

Using a table on a spreadsheet allows you to sort your data in the table.

Using the icons  you can sort the data in a column.

Select the 'Girl or Boy' column by clicking on the letter at the top of the column.

Select Sort and either Ascending or Descending.

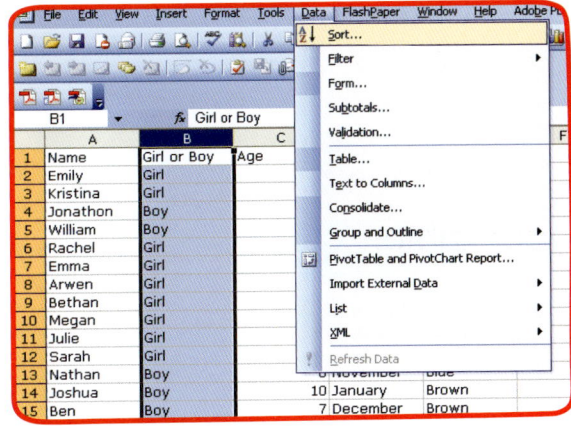

You will be asked whether you want to expand the selection.

What happens to the data if you choose yes?
What happens to the data if you choose to use just the selected data?

Which do you think you should use, and why?

What happens to the word data?
What happens to the numerical data?

 **Venn Diagrams**

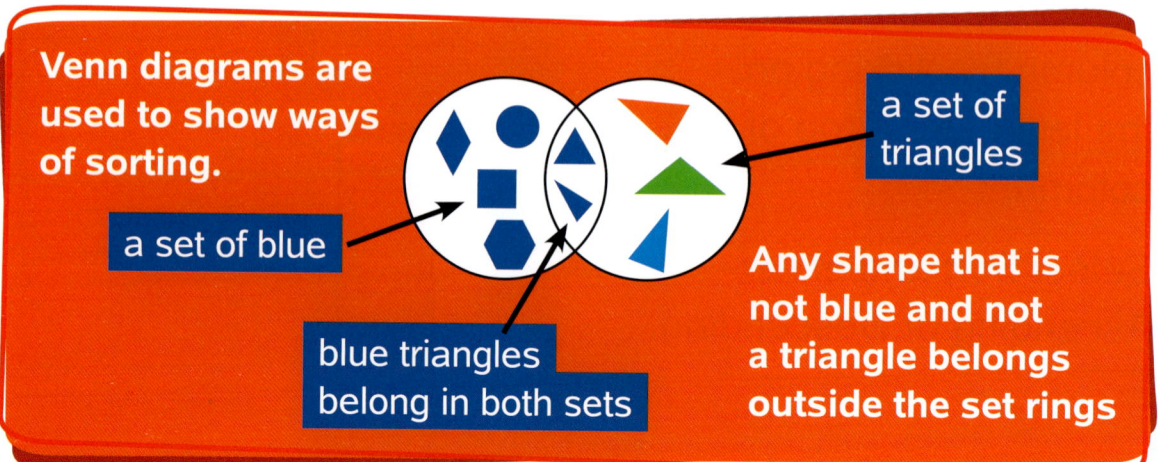

Venn diagrams are used to show ways of sorting.

a set of blue

a set of triangles

blue triangles belong in both sets

Any shape that is not blue and not a triangle belongs outside the set rings

Use a Venn diagram to sort numbers.

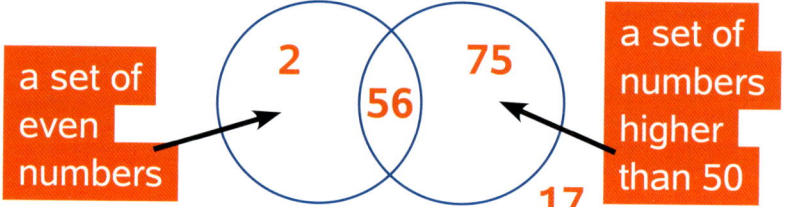

a set of even numbers

2   75
   56

17

a set of numbers higher than 50

1 Copy the Venn diagram and use it to sort out these numbers. 28, 61, 94, 35, 52, 53, 42, 9

2 Copy this Venn diagram and sort out the numbers. 27, 38, 59, 82, 67, 42, 31, 18, 4, 66

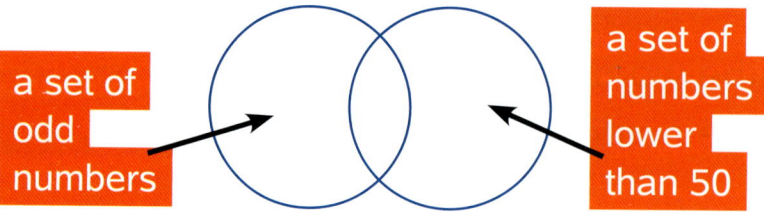

a set of odd numbers

a set of numbers lower than 50

More Venn Diagrams

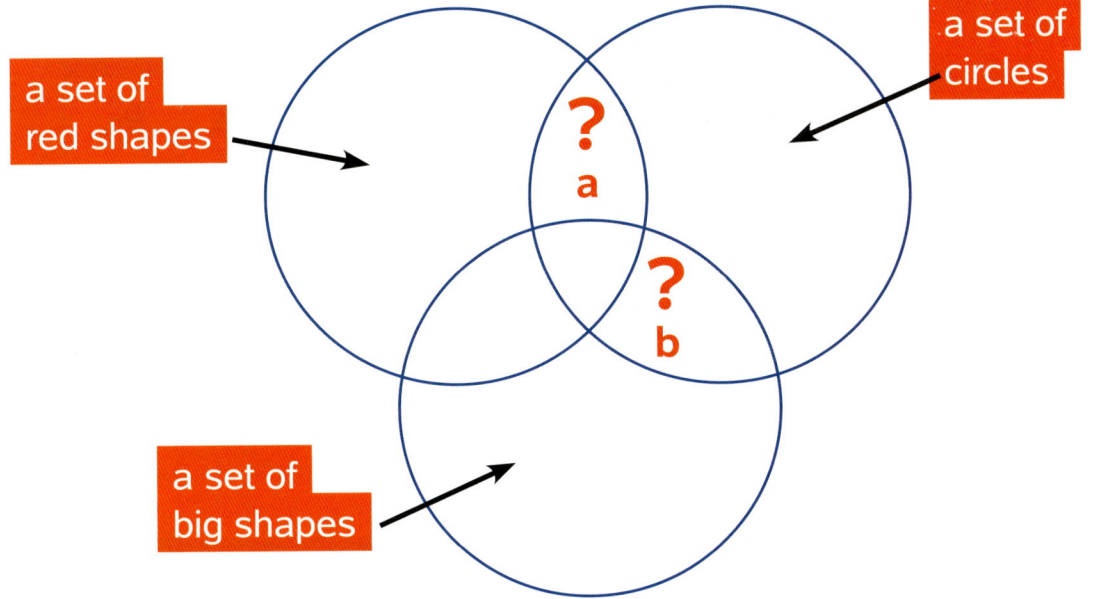

a set of
red shapes

a set of
circles

? a

? b

a set of
big shapes

Where would you put these shapes?

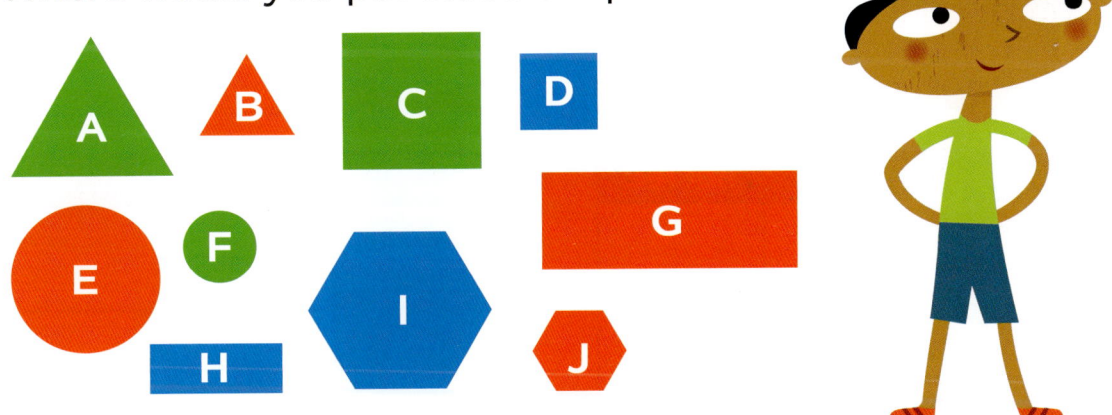

A   B   C   D

E   F   G

H   I   J

1   What shape could go in the spaces marked with 'a'?
2   What shape could go in the space marked with 'b'?
3   Copy the Venn diagram and write the letter
   of each shape in the correct space.

Carroll Diagrams

Carroll diagrams are another way of showing how things have been sorted.

	red	not red
triangles	▲	▲ ▌▟
not triangles	▬ ▐ ●	● ▬ ◆

Use a box of geometric shapes and try sorting them on each of these Carroll diagrams.

1

	blue	not blue
square		
not square		

2

	green	not green
circle		
not circle		

3

	red	not red
hexagon		
not hexagon		

4

	blue	not blue
oblong		
not oblong		

Challenge

Use a Carroll diagram to show which of the boys and which of the girls in your class are left-handed or right-handed.

Sorting Trees

Sort out all the red shapes from a box of geometric shapes.

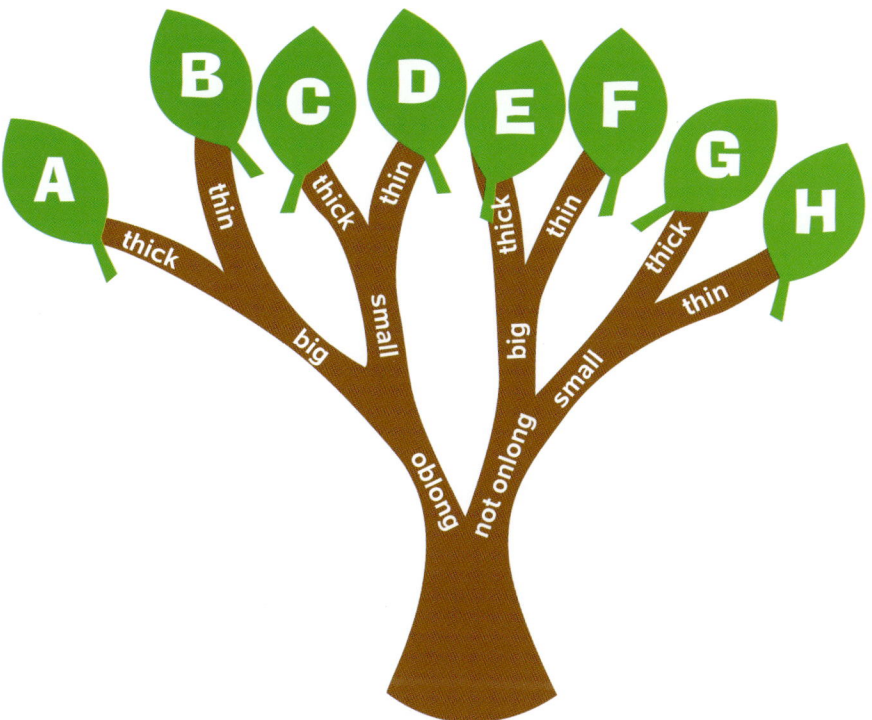

Which shapes end up in each of the leaves?

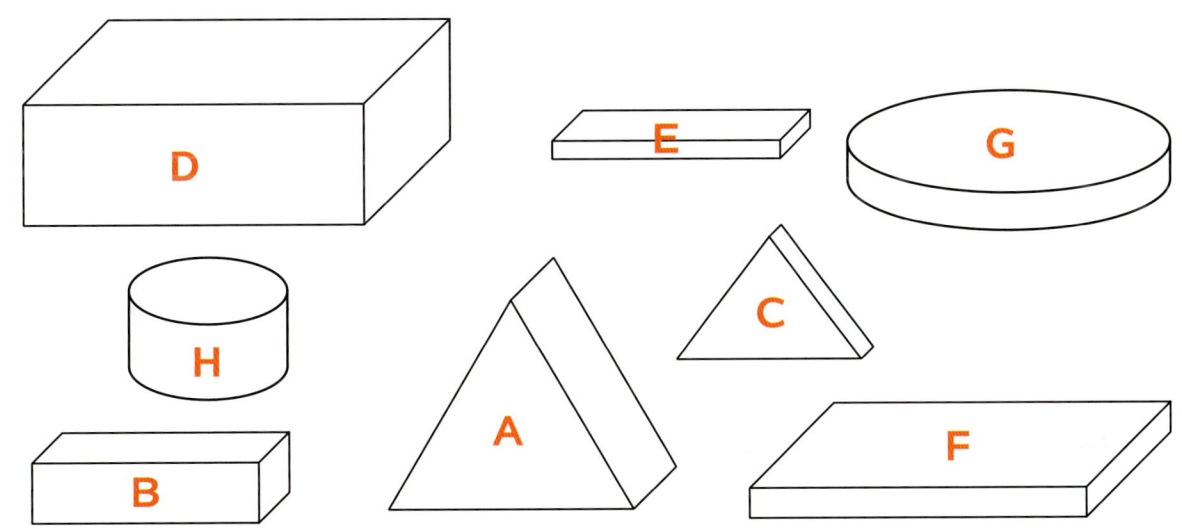

The Data Detective

The problem:

- **The school wishes to buy chairs for the library with an attached desk on one of the arms of the chair.**
- **If the desks are attached on the right hand arm this is fine for right handed pupils but not very good for the left handed pupils.**
- **If the school is going to buy a total of 30 desks, how many should have the desk on the right and how many should have the desk on the left? We know there are fewer left handed children than right handed children, but how many of each?**

Planning the Investigation

What information do you need to collect and how are you going to collect it?

Use your class as a first sample of children. Use another class to give another set of data. You could use all the classes in your school.

Consider why it is a good idea to use multiple sets of data.

Data Collection

Collect your data.

Analysis

Sort your data into a table.
Think about the headings for your columns and rows.
Look for any patterns or trends in the data.

Conclusion

Use your data to make a decision about how many chairs the school should buy with the desk on the right and how many chairs it should buy with desks on the left.

Is there any other information that may have been useful to collect to help you make a decision?

CHAPTER 30

Probability

Some things in life are certain.
'Without water you will die.'
Some things in life are impossible.
'A fish can live out of water.'
Everything else is possible — but it can be likely or unlikely.

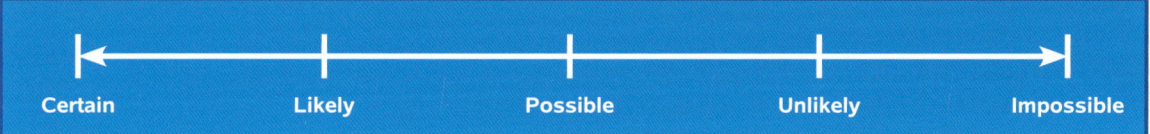

Certain   Likely   Possible   Unlikely   Impossible

Where on the probability range does each statement belong?

1   I will go to sleep tonight.
2   My teacher will be off school tomorrow.
3   My friend's dog will learn to read.
4   I will eat some lollies this week.
5   My dad will catch a fish at the weekend.

Challenge

Write a statement for each place on the probability range.

 **More Probability**

Horiana and Stephen are playing an addition and subtraction game.
These are the cards in the pile.

$+2$ -2 $+4$ $+6$ $+2$ -4 $+2$ $+2$

Use the words 'certain, likely, possible, unlikely or impossible' to describe each statement.

1 Horiana will pick an even number.
2 Stephen will pick a card with 2 on it.
3 Horiana will pick a subtraction card.
4 Stephen will pick an odd number.
5 Horiana will pick a card with 6 on it.
6 Stephen will pick an addition card.

The teacher gave them five more cards and they played the game again.
These are the cards the teacher gave them.

-3 -5 -4 -1 -3

Answer the statements 1 to 6 again for Horiana and Stephen's second game.

Rolling Dice

You will need 2 dice, both with the numbers 1 to 6. Roll both the dice.

Find the total for the roll.

5 + 4 = 9
Total = 9

Keep a record of your totals for at least 50 throws.

Suggestion: design a tally chart to keep your record.

1 What are the different totals you could get?
2 Is it more or less likely that you will roll a total of 2 rather than a total of 7?

Try to explain your answer.

Clue: how many different ways can you make each total?

Challenge

Roll 3 dice.
Which are the most likely totals?

 **Is it Fair?**

You will need 2 blank wooden cubes and two friends to play the games with.

On the first cube colour 2 faces red, 2 faces blue and 2 faces yellow. On the second cube colour 1 face red, 2 faces blue and 3 faces yellow.

Decide whether you want to be red, yellow or blue. (each person is one colour.)

Game 1

Roll the first cube 20 times and keep a record of who wins each time. (If your colour is on top you win.)
Design a table to record your results. The person who has the most wins, wins the game.

Play the game again – does the same person win?

Game 2

Roll the second cube 20 times and keep a record of who wins each time. Record your results in a table.

Play the game again – does the same person win?

In your group discuss whether the two games are fair. Does everyone have an equal chance of winning either game?

Mr Morgan's Plastic Factory

Mr Morgan's plastic factory makes 3 colours of plastic. Last summer he designed some bucket and spade sets.

handle

bucket

spade

You can use these colours or choose 3 different colours for Mr Morgan.

How many different sets could you make?

Design a chart or table to make sure you get all the possibilities.